Chicanos in Higher Education:
Issues and Dilemmas for the 21st Century

by Adalberto Aguirre, Jr., and Ruben O. Martinez

ASHE-ERIC Higher Education Report No. 3, 1993

Prepared by

Clearinghouse on Higher Education
The George Washington University

In cooperation with

ASHE

Association for the Study
of Higher Education

Published by

School of Education and Human Development
The George Washington University

Jonathan D. Fife, Series Editor

Cite as
Aguirre, Adalberto, Jr., ʹ ɹ Ruben O. Martinez. 1993. *Chicanos in Higher Education: ʃsues and Dilemmas for the 21st Century.* ASHE-ERIC Higʹıer Education Report No. 3. Washington, D.C.: The George Washington University, School of Education and Human Development.

Library of Congress Catalog Card Number 93-61673
ISSN 0884-0040
ISBN 1-878380-24-9

Managing Editor: Bryan Hollister
Manuscript Editor: Barbara Fishel, Editech
Cover design by Michael David Brown, Rockville, Maryland

The ERIC Clearinghouse on Higher Education invites individuals to submit proposals for writing monographs for the *ASHE-ERIC Higher Education Report* series. Proposals must include:
1. A detailed manuscript proposal of not more than five pages.
2. A chapter-by-chapter outline.
3. A 75-word summary to be used by several review committees for the initial screening and rating of each proposal.
4. A vita and a writing sample.

ERIC Clearinghouse on Higher Education
School of Education and Human Development
The George Washington University
One Dupont Circle, Suite 630
Washington, DC 20036-1183

This publication was prepared partially with funding from the Office of Educational Research and Improvement, U.S. Department of Education, under contract no. ED RI-88-062014. The opinions expressed in this report do not necessarily reflect the positions or policies of OERI or the Department.

EXECUTIVE SUMMARY

As we approach the 21st century, U.S. society is renewing its interest in educational opportunity for racial and ethnic minorities. Not since the civil rights movement of the 1960s have we seen stirrings in this area that seemingly promise some change in the relationship between educational institutions and ethnic minority populations. As one of the fastest-growing minority populations in the United States, the Chicano population needs to examine its educational condition in U.S. society.

How Do Chicanos Relate to the U.S. Educational System?

An educational crisis exists in the Chicano population, for the Chicano population has fared poorly in its progress through the U.S. educational system. Compared to the educational outcomes of other racial and ethnic populations in the United States, the Chicano population's educational outcomes are deplorably low. In 1990, for example, less than half of the Chicano population 25 years and older had completed at least four years of high school. Compared with other ethnic groups in the Hispanic population, the Chicano population ranks at the bottom.

Chicanos are undereducated, and a contributing factor to that undereducation is the relative social and cultural isolation of Chicanos in U.S. schools. This relative isolation, coupled with segmentation created by educational tracking, has placed the population at risk with regard to its educational outcomes and its economic outcomes. Perhaps the most noticeable feature of the Chicano population's position of risk in U.S. schools is the high dropout rate from high school of its youth.

How Do Chicanos Relate to Higher Education?

While access to higher education has improved slowly for Chicanos, the number of Chicanos in postsecondary institutions is quite low. The limited presence of Chicanos in higher education can be attributed, in part, to the small number of Chicano students who pursue a postsecondary education. The tapering of the educational pipeline results in a trickle of Chicano students entering postsecondary institutions.

The participation of Chicano students in U.S. higher education has a long and obscure history. It began with the early days of *los californios* at Santa Clara College in the 1850s and reached its zenith in the turbulence of Chicano students at Berkeley in the 1960s. The social and political climate of the 1960s served as the context for the construction of *El Plan de Santa Barbara,* in which Chicano students and community members defined the aims of higher education for themselves.

What Is the Context for Chicanos' Participation In Higher Education?

While the civil rights struggles of the 1960s were important in shaping the aims of higher education for Chicanos, the federal government was the source of support programs that facilitated the participation of Chicanos in higher education, for example, the Servicemen's Readjustment Act of 1944, the G.I. Bill of Rights, the National Defense and Education Act of 1958, the Civil Rights Act of 1964, and the Higher Education Act of 1965. These programs were the initial bridges that brought the Chicano population into institutions of higher education in relatively substantial numbers.

While they facilitated the entry of Chicanos into higher education, these programs also reinforced the subordinate status of Chicanos in U.S. society. Given their limited financial resources, Chicano students were channeled into two-year colleges, where they became victims of low transfer rates to four-year institutions and high attrition rates. Thus, the number of Chicano students at four-year institutions has been low, even lower at some more prestigious institutions of higher education.

How Are Chicanos Represented in Higher Education?

Perhaps the best indicator of the tenuous presence of Chicanos in higher education is found in an examination of Chicano faculty. Chicano faculty are often viewed as having embarked on "extraordinary careers" in the U.S. educational system, as having surpassed the expectations U.S. society ascribes to them. But does higher education recognize their extraordinary careers?

Chicano faculty, for the most part, are peripheral members of academe. On the one hand, postsecondary institutions use them to address minority concerns. On the other hand, white faculty do not regard them as legitimate participants in academe. In most cases, they are regarded as impositions brought about by litigation and social legislation. If Chicano

faculty have traveled this far to be reminded of their subordinate status in U.S. society, how can they encourage Chicano
students to embark on their own extraordinary careers?

What Does the 21st Century Hold for
The Education of Chicanos?

As the 21st century approaches, Chicanos must use educational attainment as a vehicle for social change, in particular
as the means for entering sectors of U.S. society that bestow
influence on participants. Through such a process, Chicanos
can transform their position in U.S. society from one of relative disadvantage to one of relative influence.

Perhaps the most serious challenge facing Chicanos in the
21st century is their exclusion from policy-making arenas.
Numbers alone will not push Chicanos into those arenas;
they must preface their entry into policy-making arenas by
altering their socioeconomic status in U.S. society. One pre-
requisite for altering one's opportunity for advancement is
by enhanced educational outcomes. Thus, Chicanos must
use educational attainment as a net for gathering forces in
the shaping of policy agendas.

ADVISORY BOARD

CONSULTING EDITORS

Louis C. Attinasi, Jr.
University of Houston

Beverly Belson
Western Michigan University

David W. Breneman
Harvard University

Kimberly Brown
Portland State University

L. Edwin Coate
Oregon State University

Robert Cope
Northwoods Institute

Jane F. Earley
Mankato State University

Walter H. Gmelch
Washington State University

Dennis E. Gregory
Wake Forest University

James O. Hammons
University of Arkansas

Robert M. Hendrickson
The Pennsylvania State University

Mary Ann Heverly
Delaware County Community College

Malcolm D. Hill
The Pennsylvania State University

Clifford P. Hooker
University of Minnesota

George D. Kuh
Indiana University

Sock-Foon C. MacDougall
Bowie State University

James L. Morrison
The University of North Carolina–Chapel Hill

Patricia Murrell
Memphis State University

REVIEW PANEL

Charles Adams
University of Massachusetts–Amherst

Louis Albert
American Association for Higher Education

Richard Alfred
University of Michigan

Philip G. Altbach
State University of New York–Buffalo

Marilyn J. Amey
University of Kansas

Louis C. Attinasi, Jr.
University of Houston

Robert J. Barak
Iowa State Board of Regents

Alan Bayer
Virginia Polytechnic Institute and State University

John P. Bean
Indiana University

Louis W. Bender
Florida State University

John M. Braxton
Vanderbilt University

Peter McE. Buchanan
Council for Advancement and
    Support of Education

John A. Centra
Syracuse University

Arthur W. Chickering
George Mason University

Shirley M. Clark
Oregon State System of Higher Education

Darrel A. Clowes
Virginia Polytechnic Institute and State University

John W. Creswell
University of Nebraska–Lincoln

Deborah DiCroce
Piedmont Virginia Community College

Richard Duran
University of California

Kenneth C. Green
University of Southern California

Edward R. Hines
Illinois State University

Marsha W. Krotseng
West Virginia State College and University Systems

George D. Kuh
Indiana University–Bloomington

Daniel T. Layzell
University of Wisconsin System

Meredith Ludwig
American Association of State Colleges and Universities

Mantha V. Mehallis
Florida Atlantic University

Robert J. Menges
Northwestern University

Toby Milton
Essex Community College

James R. Mingle
State Higher Education Executive Officers

Gary Rhoades
University of Arizona

G. Jeremiah Ryan
Harford Community College

Daryl G. Smith
Claremont Graduate School

William Tierney
The Pennsylvania State University

Susan Twombly
University of Kansas

Harold Wechsler
University of Rochester

Michael J. Worth
The George Washington University

CONTENTS

FOREWORD

The need to address the issues affecting Chicanos in higher
education is similar to the considerations leading to the crea-
tion of Harvard in 1636. The good people of Boston realized
that it was fundamental to their welfare to have an institution
of higher education to train citizens to be future government
leaders and ministers. They took steps to see that this education was available long before the population of Boston
reached any critical magnitude. And they did it, initially, without regard to the wealth of students' families, by using
revenues from the tolls charged for the Charles River ferry
to help support the institution.

The social and cultural isolation of Boston from England
and the rest of the colonies, its small population, and its citizens' relative lack of economic affluence are not terribly different from the experience of Chicanos today. While the cultural background of 17th century English settlers and 20th
century Chicanos are vastly different, that situation is due to
change. Not too far into the 21st century, the population of
Chicanos will grow to be as important as any other group of
people in the United States. Consequently, it is in the best
interests of all communities and educational institutions to
make the education of Chicanos a primary objective of their
mission.

For higher education, doing so means more than making
the recruitment of Chicanos an objective of the admissions
office. It means looking at this mission systematically and finding answers to the following questions:

- What role can my institution play in elementary and
  secondary schools to encourage Chicanos to attend postsecondary institutions?
- What can be done to develop better cultural congruency
  within the institution for Chicano students?
- What will create a greater understanding by faculty of the
  educational expectations and learning styles of Chicanos?
- What courses must be added to the curriculum?

Answers to such questions would help to make the educational process more sensitive and effective.

In this report, Adalberto Aguirre, Jr., associate professor of
sociology at the University of California–Riverside, and Ruben
O. Martinez, chair of the Department of Sociology and president of the Faculty Assembly at the University of Colorado–

Colorado Springs, discuss the context for the education of Chicanos and the issues affecting Chicanos' access to post-secondary education. They consider the current and future undergraduate experience, enrollment patterns, and career paths of Chicano students. They also look at dilemmas in academe for Chicano faculty, including institutional stratification.

The objective of all colleges should be to attract students who can benefit from the education being offered and to have a process that will allow every student to achieve his or her highest education potential—which does not means lowering standards or inflating grades. It does mean gaining a better understanding about the real mission of education, how the procedures of the institution relate to each other, and the different impacts these interrelationships have on students. This report will help administrators and faculty understand better what they might mean for their Chicano students.

Jonathan D. Fife
Series Editor, Professor, and
Director, ERIC Clearinghouse on Higher Education

PREFACE AND ACKNOWLEDGMENTS

We have purposely avoided defining the term "Chicano." The majority of Chicano scholars would argue that such an attempt would be monumental, and the term "Chicano" has too many critical aspects—ideological and political—to address, which would result in a different topic for this monograph. We do not pretend to know the definition of the term.

By not defining "Chicano," however, we are not taking the easy way out of a serious discussion. Rather, we recognize the seriousness by not attempting to construct a definition for purely utilitarian reasons. We suspect that some readers might feel uncomfortable with our use of the term "Chicano" to identify a population that consists of persons of Mexican origin, whether born in the United States or in Mexico. While we recognize the uncritical use of "Chicano," we also recognize one aspect of the reality surrounding persons of Mexican origin in the United States: that popular thinking among whites in the United States does not distinguish between Chicanos and Mexicans. They are regarded as all the same.

We have benefited from the advice of several persons in writing this monograph, among them Ray Padilla, Hisauro Garza, Tomas Arciniega, Gloria Cuadraz, Richard Verdugo, and Dennis Bixler. We were also lucky to have had the opportunity to participate in two institutional activities focused on issues and concerns related to higher education for Chicanos: the PEW manuscript project at the Tomas Rivera Center under the direction of Arturo Madrid and Ray Garza, and the IUP research forum organized by Michael Olivas at the University of Houston. In addition, the opportunity to share a cup of coffee with Michael Olivas in Washington, D.C., over a decade ago resulted in the growth of the idea for this monograph. The ERIC Clearinghouse staff was invaluable in providing us with extensive research and resource materials. We are happy, too, to have had the opportunity to share some of the ideas in this monograph with the late Tomas Rivera. Finally, we thank our families for their support and encouragement.

THE EDUCATION OF CHICANOS

Several years ago, the first Chicano chancellor at a University of California campus observed that the Chicano community:

No longer does a potential educational crisis exist in the Chicano population: It is clearly here today.

> . . . *is not developing as well as other elements within American society. It needs leadership in all areas. It has problems and situations that need short- and long-range attention and solutions . . . [a fact] well known by Chicanos and non-Chicanos. Only the Native American ranks lower than the Chicano in educational achievement at the elementary, secondary, and higher education levels, and in the ability to aggregate material wealth as well as physical and mental well-being* (Rivera 1982, p. 77).

A report prepared by the Chicano/Latino Consortium at the University of California regarding the education of Chicanos in California expresses similar concern:

> *Despite their numbers, they remain conspicuously underrepresented in the recognized areas of power and influence. When compared to other ethnic groups, their numbers in the areas of government, education, business, science, health, and the legal profession are deplorably low. . . . If Chicanos/Latinos continue to be poorly served by the educational process, as they have in the past, the problem will escalate* (1988, p. 1).

No longer does a potential educational crisis exist in the Chicano population: It is clearly here today. The large number of Chicanos in the population has not only enhanced the population's visibility within U.S. society; it has also drawn attention to the population's low levels of educational attainment. As the Chicano population's growth has been coupled with low levels of educational attainment, a cycle of educational inequality has developed in the Chicano population that is a direct challenge to social and public policy in the 1990s.

If, for example, the Chicano population continues its pattern of low educational attainment in the 1990s, at a time when the majority of the white population moves closer to retirement age, then the Chicano population will be constrained in its acquisition of educational credentials. In particular, the population will be constrained in its acquisition of educational credentials beyond secondary school that are necessary for entry into careers and professions (Aguirre and

Martinez 1984), with a result that Chicano workers will not enter occupations that can promote Chicanos' role in a vibrant economy (California Legislature 1985). That is, despite increasing numbers in the U.S. population, the Chicano population will not be distributed across occupations that could enable it to play an important economic role in the 21st century.

The Chicano population's economic role in the 21st century becomes even more important when one considers that Chicano students will represent a significant school-age population in the 21st century. The Chicano population's limited occupational mobility, however, will limit the population's ability to influence educational funding, especially state-level funding. Further, Chicanos will need to increase their entry into careers and professions to develop and promote support for educational programs in the 21st century. If not, the 21st century will only worsen the Chicano population's educational situation at a time when Chicano students will represent a significant proportion of the enrollment in schools.

It is time to reexamine the educational condition of the Chicano population, particularly those features that typify educational outcomes in the Chicano population and the context for its educational growth, especially at the postsecondary level. This section therefore provides an overview of the educational outcomes and issues that typify the educational condition of the Chicano population.

Population Change

The U.S. population is undergoing a major demographic change. The growth of ethnic minority populations is rapidly transforming them into majority components of the country's population. By 2000, one-third of the U.S. population could consist of nonwhite minorities (Griffith, Frase, and Ralph 1989). In California, where nonwhite minority populations, especially Asians and Chicanos, are growing rapidly, nonwhite minorities are expected to constitute slightly more than half of California's population by 2000 (California Legislature 1985; Hayes-Bautista, Schink, and Chapa 1988; Hyland 1992). Ironically, we are moving toward a situation where the numerical majority is a socially oppressed minority.

According to table 1, the Chicano population increased in both number and representation in the U.S. population from 1960 to 1990. The U.S. population increased 37 percent during that period, while the Chicano population increased more than sixfold, or about 530 percent. Further, between 1960 and 1990 the Chicano population's representation in the U.S. population increased 350 percent. The numerical increase in Chicanos will be felt most in the Southwest, where slightly more than 80 percent of the Chicano population resides (U.S. Bureau of the Census 1991d). Readers should keep this growth in the Chicano population in context to be better able to interpret the social and public policy issues surrounding educational concerns among Chicanos.

TABLE 1
THE CHICANO POPULATION: 1960 to 1990
(Millions)

	Total U.S. Population	Chicano Population	Chicano Population as Percent of U.S. Population
1960	179.3	2.1	1.2
1970	203.2	5.8	2.9
1980	226.5	8.7	3.8
1990	246.2	13.3	5.4

Source: U.S. Bureau of the Census 1963, 1973, 1982, 1991b.

Chicanos and the Educational Pipeline
The Chicano population has fared poorly in its progress through the U.S. educational system. When contrasted with the educational outcomes of the white population, the educational outcomes of the Chicano population are deplorably low. The data in table 2 lead to the following observations for the educational outcomes of Chicanos:

1. The proportion of persons completing more years of formal schooling has increased.
2. The proportion of persons completing four or more years of high school has increased the most.
3. The proportion of persons completing four or more years of college has increased the least.

Despite the substantial gains between 1975 and 1990 in the proportion of Chicanos completing four or more years of high school, less than half of the Chicano population had completed at least four years of high school in 1990.

TABLE 2
EDUCATIONAL ATTAINMENT OF WHITES AND CHICANOS
25 YEARS AND OLDER: 1975 to 1990

	Percent Completed Fewer Than Five Years of School		Percent Completed Four Years or More of High School		Percent Completed Four Years or More of College	
	White	*Chicano*	*White*	*Chicano*	*White*	*Chicano*
1975	4.3	24.6	62.6	30.9	14.1	3.4
1980	3.2	20.1	69.6	38.1	17.4	4.9
1985	2.7	17.1	73.9	41.9	22.4	5.5
1990	1.7	15.5	79.6	44.1	22.2	5.4

Source: U.S. Bureau of the Census 1976, 1982, 1985, 1991b.

The educational outcomes observed in table 2 illustrate the tapering of Chicanos' educational attainment at the secondary and postsecondary levels. That is, the number of Chicano students tends to decrease as they progress farther within the U.S. educational system, especially at the postsecondary level. The educational pipeline for Chicanos has been characterized as follows:

> *Beginning with a cohort of 100 students, only 55 Chicanos . . . will graduate from high school, compared with 83 white students and 72 blacks. Of the 100, only 22 Chicanos . . . will enroll in an institution of higher education, compared with 38 whites and 29 blacks. Only seven Chicanos . . . out of 100 will complete college, compared with 23 whites and 12 blacks* (de los Santos 1984, p. 82).

Chicanos, Puerto Ricans, and Cubans
When compared with the educational outcomes of other ethnic groups in the Hispanic population, the educational outcomes of the Chicano population are still quite low. Table 3 shows, for example, that the educational outcomes of the Chicano population in general are similar to those of the Puerto Rican population, but different from those of the Cuban population. Cubans made greater relative gains between 1980 and 1990 at the high school level than either Chicanos or Puerto Ricans, and only the Chicano population did not have a majority completing at least four years of high school in 1990. At the college level, Cubans and Puerto Ricans, but not Chicanos, made relative aggregate gains between 1980 and 1990.

TABLE 3
EDUCATIONAL ATTAINMENT BY ETHNIC POPULATION
25 YEARS AND OLDER: 1980 to 1990

	Percent Completed Fewer Than Five Years of School			Percent Completed Four Years or More of High School			Percent Completed Four Years or More of College		
	1980	1985	1990	1980	1985	1990	1980	1985	1990
Chicano	20.1	17.1	15.5	38.1	41.9	44.1	4.9	5.5	5.4
Cuban	7.3	7.4	5.8	44.6	51.1	63.5	12.2	13.7	20.2
Puerto Rican	14.1	12.8	9.7	45.9	46.3	55.5	5.6	7.0	9.7

Source: U.S. Bureau of the Census 1982, 1985, 1991b.

The differential pattern of educational outcomes in table
3 for the ethnic groups in the Hispanic population can be put
in context, in part, by understanding the level of social, occupational, and economic integration of each group in U.S. society. Three factors are significant in setting the Cuban population's presence in the United States apart from that of the
Puerto Rican and Chicano populations:

> *First, the early immigrants were primarily political rather
> than economic refugees. Second, . . . individuals from pro-
> fessional, urban, and more highly educated sectors were
> greatly overrepresented. Third, their reception in this country
> was not the tacit acceptance by employers hungry for
> cheap labor but rather a public welcome by the federal gov-
> ernment eager to harbor those seeking refuge from a Com-
> munist dictatorship* (Bean and Tienda 1987, p. 28).

As a result, the high levels of educational attainment in the
Cuban population have been associated with the population's
greater share of the middle class than either the Puerto Rican
or Chicano populations (Ortiz 1986). Within this context,
then, the educational outcomes in table 3 could reflect a
greater relative cost for Chicano and Puerto Rican ethnicity
than for Cuban ethnicity in the United States (Arce 1981;
Bonilla and Campos 1981).

Other ethnic minority populations
Table 4 shows how the educational outcomes of the Chicano
population in 1980 and 1990 contrast with the educational
outcomes of other racial and ethnic populations in the United

TABLE 4
SCHOOLING COMPLETED BY RACE/ETHNICITY
FOR PERSONS 25 YEARS AND OLDER

	Percent Completed Four Years or More of High School		Percent Completed Four Years or More of College	
	1980	*1990*	*1980*	*1990*
Asian	74.5	80.4	32.9	39.9
White	69.6	79.1	17.4	28.5
African-American	51.2	65.5	8.4	11.4
Puerto Rican	45.9	55.5	5.6	9.7
Cuban	44.6	63.5	12.2	20.2
Chicano	38.1	44.1	4.9	5.4

Sources: Suzuki 1989; Thomas and Hirsch 1989; U.S. Bureau of the Census 1982, 1991a, 1991b, 1992.

States (not including Native Americans). Compared with the other racial and ethnic populations, the Chicano population had the lowest high school and college completion rates in 1980 and 1990. In contrast, the Asian population ranked at the top on both high school and college completion rates.

The contrast between the educational outcomes of the Asian population and the Chicano population becomes alarming when one considers that the Asian population accounted for 1.6 percent of the U.S. population in 1980 and 2.9 percent in 1990 and the Chicano population accounted for 3.8 percent of the U.S. population in 1980 and 5.4 percent in 1990. Given their relative population size, the Asian population's high educational achievement clearly overshadows the low educational achievement of the Chicano population. In addition, the relative overeducation of the Asian population is enhanced when contrasted with the educational outcomes of the white population.

Despite the rather gloomy portrait of the Chicano population's educational condition created by the data in tables 2 to 4, the data do support the observations of several researchers that the high school noncompletion rate for Chicanos varies from 40 to 50 percent (Fernandez and Shu 1988; Negrete 1981; Valverde 1987) and that less than 10 percent of the persons in the Chicano population are earning college degrees (Committee on Education and Labor 1984; Cortese 1985; Medina 1988; Payan, Peterson, and Castille 1984). Thus, one can assume that the data in tables 2 to 4 reliably characterize the educational condition of the Chicano population.

The Context for Education of Chicanos

Though it is not the intent of this monograph to undertake a comprehensive review of the social and historical factors that have shaped the education of Chicanos in the United States, it must be noted that at least one dimension continues to play a significant role in the educational outcomes of Chicanos: *isolation*. In this discussion, "isolation" refers to educational processes, such as tracking, and dimensions of social structure, such as residential segregation, that result in the dislocation of Chicano students in the allocation of educational opportunity (Carter and Segura 1979; Gonzalez 1990; Negrete 1981; San Miguel 1987). For example, the residential segregation experienced by Chicano students results in their concentration in low-income minority schools characterized by low levels of educational attainment (Orfield 1989). As a result, Chicano students become dislocated in a system of educational opportunity that links academic preparation with extended education. In this sense, then, Chicano students are isolated in the U.S. educational system. It is not surprising to find that Chicano students are labeled "disadvantaged" in an educational system that expands, rather than reduces, Chicano students' isolation.

> *More than anyone else, [Chicano students have] been studied and tested and retested by social scientists, educators, and psychometrists. The sad truth of the matter is that all this studying and testing [have] not basically changed the position of the disadvantaged pupil in American society, and in some cases it has hurt more than helped* (Brischetto and Arciniega 1973, pp. 23–24).

Thus, the isolation of Chicano students in the educational system has fostered a context of neglect that serves to segregate Chicano students from educational opportunity.

Educational isolation

In 1971, the U.S. Commission on Civil Rights published a report, *Ethnic Isolation of Mexican Americans in the Public Schools of the Southwest*, examining the degree to which Chicano students and teachers were segregated in southwestern schools. The report had three principal findings:

1. Thirty percent of the Chicano students in the Southwest attended schools in which they accounted for 50 percent or more of the school's total enrollment.
2. Chicano teachers were significantly underrepresented among teachers and were most often found in schools with large enrollments of Chicano students.
3. Chicanos were underrepresented on local boards of education.

In general, the commission's report was significant for the education of Chicanos for at least two reasons. First, the report identified educational segregation as a constraint on Chicano students' access to educational opportunity. Second, the report identified educational inequality as a contributing factor to Chicanos' social and economic inequality in the Southwest.

Isolation and educational inequality

The association between educational isolation and educational inequality has raised questions about the cultural and structural accommodation in U.S. schools of students who are victims of social and economic inequality (Aguirre 1980; Duran 1983, *Forthcoming*; Haro 1977a; Valencia 1984). The most critical aspect of the association between isolation and inequality is its focus on structural features in the school and their association with academic achievement. For example, the educational isolation of Chicano students in school is directly related to their academic achievement. An analysis of CAP (California Assessment Program) reading data found a negative association between testing in a score quartile and proportion of Chicano students in a school (Espinosa and Ochoa 1986). That is, Chicano students who scored in the lower quartiles were more likely to attend segregated schools—schools in which Chicano students made up the majority of the school's enrollment. One must be cautious, however, when interpreting the association between isolation and inequality:

> *Although correlational data do not imply causality, it is safe to assume that segregation is a key institutional process in the denial of equal educational opportunity for Chicano students* (Menchaca and Valencia 1990, p. 223).

Thus, aside from its potential causal effects, isolation in the form of segregation is a contextual feature of the Chicano student's structured relationship to the school. Isolation, in this sense, is more of a contributing factor that might not necessarily direct the outcomes of school structure. Rather, isolation serves to create a context that facilitates certain outcomes for school structure.

The cost of isolation

The cost of educational isolation for Chicano students, especially in elementary schools, has been identified as lower self-esteem and reluctance to participate in the dominant society (Arevalo and Brown 1983; Trueba 1990), lower educational attainment as measured by standardized tests (Aguirre 1979; Humphreys 1988), placement in low-ability tracks (England, Meier, and Fraga 1988; Espinosa and Ochoa 1986), and underpreparation in some academic content areas (Duran 1983; O'Malley 1987). The cumulative effect of educational isolation for Chicano students can be observed in the undereducation of the Chicano population. In turn, from the point of view of social systems, the undereducation of the Chicano population serves to reinforce the subordinate position of the population within the country's opportunity structure.

The secondary school context

The cost of educational isolation increases for Chicano students at the middle and high school levels, where they are tracked into low-ability academic subjects and general/vocational education classes. Despite the lack of evidence that tracking benefits academic achievement (Sorensen and Hallinan 1986), Chicano students in middle schools and high schools find themselves tracked into curricula that promote their educational inequality (Aguirre 1980; Oakes 1985). For example, tracking Chicano middle and high school students into low-ability academic subjects promotes their educational inequality by not providing them with enough exposure to an academic subject to acquire the background necessary for doing well on standardized tests like the SAT, by focusing on rote or memorizing rather than critical thinking skills, especially writing ability, and by not providing them with skills in math that would enable them to proceed into higher-order mathematics beyond the basics. It is therefore not surprising to find that Chicano middle and high school students are tracked into academic subjects that promote their educational inequality by not providing them with an educational environment and educational curriculum that prepare them for study at the postsecondary level (Oakes 1986a, 1986b; Valdivieso 1986). In a sense, Chicano students are exposed to educational processes with terminal outcomes.

Segmentation

The effects from the segmentation of Chicano middle and high school students into tracks that promote their educational inequality have been observed as lower self-esteem, negative feelings toward school, lack of motivation, and high absenteeism from classes (Medina 1988). The segmentation of Chicano students into low-ability tracks also places them in a peripheral relationship to a school's distribution of educational opportunity. This peripheral relationship of Chicano students in turn enables the school to use school structure to maintain them in a peripheral relationship by arguing that Chicano students are either *uninterested, uneducable, or not academically motivated.* Even the most peripheral Chicano students—Chicano gang members—are not alienated from educational objectives (Schwartz 1989). That is, what alienates Chicano students from educational objectives is the expectations created for them through school structure. Thus, the segmentation of Chicano middle and high school students becomes an institutional vehicle legitimating the expectations for Chicano students created by school structure. One of those expectations is that Chicano students will pursue educational careers only to the extent that it reproduces their social class position in U.S. society, that is, that Chicano students will accept terminal educational outcomes as a basis for defining their quality of life.

An educational dilemma

The concomitant effects of educational isolation and educational segmentation for Chicano students have been instrumental in creating an educational dilemma—an alarmingly high dropout rate for Chicano students in high school. As shown in table 2, less than half of the Chicano population 25 years old and older had completed at least four years of high school in 1990. While it is difficult to identify a causal factor or dimension that accounts for the high dropout rate of Chicano high school students, several features of Chicano dropouts have been identified (Ekstrom et al. 1987; Haro 1977b; Hiramo-Nakamishi 1986; Martinez 1986; Steinberg, Blinde, and Chan 1984; Valdivieso 1986): low grades, high absenteeism and suspension rates, and overage. Interestingly, each of these features is also found in educational contexts characterized by educational isolation and educational segmentation for Chicano students.

While the high school dropout rate is too high for the Chicano population, it is not a recent phenomenon. Almost 20 years ago, a review of Chicano education in the Southwest noted:

> *While increasingly more and more Mexican American youth are staying in school, it is true that in the southwestern United States the dropout rate is higher among them than among other minority and Anglo youth* . . . (Thornburg and Grinder 1975, pp. 357–58).

In general, since the early 1960s, the high school dropout rate for Chicano students has not dropped below 50 percent (Manuel 1965; Thornburg 1974; Ulibarri 1972; U.S. Commission on Civil Rights 1972). As a result, high school noncompletion is a chronic feature in the Chicano population's educational condition.

High school noncompletion is a chronic feature in the Chicano population's educational condition.

Continuing educational isolation

Despite the findings of the U.S. Civil Rights Commission over two decades ago regarding the segregation of Chicano students in the Southwest, Chicano students remain segregated in today's schools. And it appears that the segregation of Chicano students has increased over the last two decades. In 1968, for example, about 30 percent of the Chicano students in the Southwest attended schools in which they were more than 50 percent of the school's enrollment. By 1984, almost 70 percent of the Chicano students in the Southwest attended schools in which nonwhite minorities accounted for over 50 percent of the total enrollment, with 30 percent of those students attending schools in which nonwhite minorities were more than 90 percent of the total enrollment (Medina 1988; Orfield, Montfort, and George 1987; Orum 1986). A study based on an analysis of school enrollment patterns in southern California, where the largest concentration of Chicanos in the United States is found, noted that:

*Between 1970 and 1984, the number of whites in the
schools of typical Latino students dropped from 45 percent
to 17 percent in Los Angeles County, from 73 percent to 31
percent in Orange County, and from 63 percent to 40 percent in the Riverside and San Bernardino County area . . .*
(Orfield 1989, p. 55).

Thus, the educational isolation of Chicano students in schools
continues in general to increase. A context of increasing educational isolation will have detrimental effects on any efforts
focused on improving the educational outcomes of Chicano
students—especially when their numbers are growing rapidly.

The Postsecondary Context for Chicanos

Chicano students' dropping out of high school has attracted
considerable attention, even as the impact of a growing Chicano population is percolating upward toward postsecondary
education (Estrada 1988). Observers are concerned that if
the present rate of high school noncompletion continues in
the Chicano population and the population of Chicanos aged
five to 17 increases 30 percent by 2000 as population experts
predict, then by 2000 the number of Chicanos who have not
completed high school will represent a sizable and formidable
proportion of the Chicano population (Hayes-Bautista, Schink,
and Chapa 1988; Usdan 1984). By 2000, then, the proportion
of college-educated Chicanos will not increase appreciably.
By 2000, it is quite likely that the Chicano population will be
characterized as inadequately and inappropriately educated.

Entry into postsecondary institutions

The unequal educational opportunities encountered by Chicanos in U.S. schools have created a context in which Chicano
college applicants tend to have lower high school grade point
averages and lower scores on standardized tests than their
white counterparts (Duran 1983; Humphreys 1988). Table
5, for example, shows the contrast in SAT scores between
college-bound Chicano high school students and other
college-bound high school students by racial and ethnic background. Relative to the other racial and ethnic groups, average
SAT scores, both verbal and math, for Chicano students were
lower than those for white and Asian students. The largest
relative gains in average SAT scores, both verbal and math,
between 1975–76 and 1988–89, however, took place among
African-American and Chicano students.

TABLE 5
AVERAGE SAT SCORES FOR COLLEGE-BOUND
HIGH SCHOOL SENIORS BY RACE/ETHNICITY

	1975-76	1980-81	1984-85	1988-89
Verbal*				
All Students	431	424	431	427
White	451	442	449	446
African-American	332	332	346	351
Chicano	371	373	382	381
Asian	414	397	404	409
Math*				
All Students	472	466	475	476
White	493	483	490	491
African-American	354	362	376	386
Chicano	410	415	426	430
Asian	518	513	518	525
Combined				
All Students	903	890	906	903
White	944	925	939	937
African-American	686	694	722	737
Chicano	781	788	808	811
Asian	932	910	922	934

*Possible scores range from 200 to 800.

Source: National Center for Education Statistics 1991b.

Academic survival and continuity

It is not clear that scores on standardized tests, such as the SAT, are valid or the sole indicators of how a student will fare in college (Lunneborg and Lunneborg 1986; Willie 1987). Studies that have examined the retention rate of Chicano college students, for example, suggest that personal, nonacademic qualities, such as self-esteem, leadership ability, and community involvement, are better predictors for their persistence in college than their scores on standardized tests (Arbona and Novy 1990; Chacon, Cohen, and Strover 1986; Duran 1986; Frazier and DeBlassie 1982; Pennock-Roman 1988; Young 1992). Studies of Chicanas pursuing graduate or professional degrees found that Chicanas identified their parents' work ethic, a strong maternal role model, and strong emotional support in the family as factors that motivated them to complete such degrees (Gandara 1980, 1982).

Not only did subjects emphasize the work models of their parents, but they rated hard work and persistence in themselves as characteristics . . . they considered to be substantially more important than their own ability (Gandara 1980, p. 3).

Similarly, a study of Chicano academic personnel noted three factors underlying respondents' pursuit of a college education: strong family and parental support, the perception of college as a personal challenge, and well-defined educational goals and interests (Astin and Burciaga 1981). A study of Chicanas who were enrolled in or had completed a doctoral program noted that the majority of respondents identified the need to do well in college to show gratitude for their parents' hard work as a critical factor in their college education (Cuadraz 1989).

Unlike middle-class students, whose attainment of postsecondary education is perceived as a continuation of their parents' achievements and lifestyle, for these Chicanas, acquiring an education instead represented the opportunity to take advantage of opportunities their parents had not had. It meant doing "good" by the sacrifices their parents had made in order for them *to have better opportunities* (Cuadraz 1989, p. 12).

These studies suggest that, to understand the educational pursuits of Chicano students at the postsecondary level, one must examine contextual dimensions like the family support network rather than traditional features, such as scores on standardized tests and high school GPA—which is not to say that standardized tests and high school GPA are not important dimensions in the educational process. Rather, to understand Chicanos' pursuit of a postsecondary education, one must examine nontraditional factors that motivate students to overcome their educational inequality and result in their completion of a college degree (Cortese 1992a; Fiske 1988; Madrid 1988; Vasquez 1982).

The postsecondary pipeline
It has become increasingly difficult to isolate the results of Chicanos' postsecondary education, because "Chicano" has been incorporated into general descriptors of the ethnic pop-

TABLE 6
SELECTED CHARACTERISTICS OF CHICANO STUDENTS
IN INSTITUTIONS OF HIGHER EDUCATION

Enrollment by Type of Institution	Enrollment* (Fall 1988)
Public	
Four-Year	36.8%
Two-Year	63.2%
Private	
Four-Year	99.9%
Two-Year	0.1%

Degrees Earned by Field of Study	Associate Degrees* (1986-87)	Bachelor's Degrees* (1986-87)	Doctoral Degrees* (1987-88)
Education	28%	26%	33%
Physical Sciences	5%	5%	10%
Social Sciences	17%	34%	25%

*Estimated 60 percent of Hispanic population.
Source: National Center for Education Statistics 1991c.

ulation, such as "Hispanic" (Muñoz 1989). The inclusion of
Chicano students in the category "Hispanic" has resulted in
a lack of reliable data sets for Chicano students' postsecondary
work (Olivas 1979, 1982, 1984). In an attempt to extrapolate
postsecondary educational data for Chicano students, researchers have used a population estimate based on the proportionate representation of the Chicano population within
the Hispanic population (Astin 1982; Astin and Burciaga 1981).

While this approach provides the researcher with an approx-
imate set of baseline data for Chicano students at the postsecondary level, one must be cautious when interpreting the
representativeness of the Chicano student population. In particular, the number of Chicano students at the postsecondary
level might not be comparable to the Chicano population's
proportionate representation in the Hispanic population. If
the educational outcomes presented in table 3 are reliable
and accurate, then the number of Chicano students at the
postsecondary level extrapolated from the number of Hispanic
students at the postsecondary level will *overestimate* rather
than *underestimate* the population of Chicano students. That
is, a population estimate based on a ratio is more likely to

overestimate a population, as it includes a wider range of persons in its estimate because they are *expected* to exist.

Given these conceptual limitations for the data in table 6, one can make two general observations about postsecondary Chicano students. First, the majority of Chicano college students in fall 1988 were enrolled at two-year public colleges (de los Santos 1978; de los Santos, Montemayor, and Solis 1983; Olivas 1979). In contrast, almost all Chicano students enrolled in private institutions were in four-year colleges. Second, Chicano students tended to earn degrees in two areas: education and the social sciences (Brown et al. 1980; Chacon 1982; de los Santos 1984; Gandara 1986; Olivas 1979; Thomas 1992).

Summary
The Chicano population faces an educational crisis. Educational outcomes for Chicanos lag behind those of other racial and ethnic populations in the United States, and educational isolation continues to be a salient feature in Chicanos' educational outcomes. The increasing isolation of Chicano students in the U.S. school system and their segmentation in secondary schools into low-ability tracks could contribute to an alarmingly high dropout rate from secondary schools. To evaluate the persistence of Chicanos in postsecondary schools, one must examine nontraditional factors, such as family networks, instead of relying solely on standardized test scores or high school GPAs.

CHICANOS' ACCESS TO HIGHER EDUCATION

Chicano students' participation in U.S. institutions of higher learning has a long but obscure history. From the early days of *los californios* at Santa Clara College in the 1850s to the turbulent experiences of Chicano students at the University of California–Berkeley in the 1960s to the debates about political correctness and ideological conflicts of the 1990s, Chicanos have been underrepresented in U.S. colleges and universities (Leon and McNeill 1985; McKevitt 1990–91). During the last century, access to institutions of higher education has improved for Chicano students as a result of numerous civil rights acts, the struggles of Chicano and Chicana students, faculty, and community members for programs and centers relevant to Chicanos, and progressive institutional initiatives and responses to provide equal educational opportunity. This section discusses the Chicano student movement and its relationship to higher education, affirmative action and support practices for students, the development of departments, programs, and centers in Chicano studies, and Chicanos' educational achievement.

The Chicano Student Movement and Higher Education

The Chicano student movement of the 1960s and early 1970s traces its roots to the conflict that emerged between the United States and Mexico during the middle of the last century. The racial and ethnic dynamics set in motion by the Spaniards three centuries earlier were significantly altered by the American-Mexican War of 1846 to 1848. The takeover of the northern half of Mexico by the United States resulted in the political and economic displacement of those Mexicans who remained on their native lands. Their descendants, Mexican Americans, were raised, socialized, and constrained as members of a subordinate group within a racial society.

During the 1960s, the racial situation in the United States exploded into widespread civil unrest involving members of ethnic minority groups and the dominant group. African-Americans, Chicanos, Native Americans, and other oppressed groups called for changes in U.S. society that would include other U.S. citizens in economic, political, and cultural achievement. The Chicano student movement included mostly high school and college students and faculty; it was most intense in California, although its impact was felt throughout the Southwest and the Midwest (Gomez-Quinoñes 1978). The movement was part of the youth rebellion that became a significant political force in the 1960s but was distinct in articulating an ethnic identity for Mexican Americans and the needs of their communities (Muñoz 1989).

MEChA

Armed with an ideology of nationalism, *El Plan Espiritual de Aztlan,* and *El Plan de Santa Barbara,* Chicano students, faculty, and community members worked to improve Mexican Americans' access to colleges and universities in California and to increase the relevance of the curricula for Chicano communities. Following a conference organized by the Chicano Coordinating Council on Higher Education (CCHE) at Santa Barbara, California, in spring 1969, Chicano student organizations began to adopt the name *El Movimiento Estudiantil Chicano de Aztlan* (MEChA).

MEChA and other Chicano student organizations were instrumental in the establishment of Chicano studies and Mexican American academic and research units and student support programs at colleges and universities throughout the country. Chicano students pressured university faculty and officials to supplement the curriculum with courses on Chicanos and to implement recruitment and retention programs targeting Chicanos. Today, MEChA chapters organize statewide and national meetings and conferences that focus on the status of Chicanos and their relationship to U.S. institutions. In addition, MEChA units hold student meetings as part of the annual conference of the National Association for Chicano Studies, the official professional organization for Chicano studies.

More recently, the Hispanic Association of Colleges and Universities (HACU) has emerged as a strong voice articulating the educational needs of Chicanos and other Hispanic populations. This organization is comprised mostly of administrators from colleges and universities with significant numbers of Hispanic and Latino students. While Chicano students might no longer have a strong influence on the relationship between Chicanos and higher education, the first significant group of Chicanos to have served careers in higher education is beginning to exert its own influence.

Chicanos, civil rights, and higher education

Violations of Chicanos' civil rights by institutions of higher education were not highly evident before the 1950s, mostly because of ideology and the cumulative effects of the U.S. educational system. The "society of affluence" was not principally concerned with racism and discrimination in the postwar years. *Sputnik* and other achievements in space were central icons in the country's consciousness, not the poverty and educational inequality of Chicanos. Early in the 1960s, Chicanos did not make it out of high schools in acceptable numbers, and they certainly did not arrive at the gates of the Ivory Tower in visible numbers. Indeed, the relationship between Chicanos and institutions of higher education was so well hidden that it did not even begin to receive systematic scholarly treatment until later in the 1960s.

Student movements in the United States seemed to peak in 1968, the year that thousands of Mexican American students walked out of classes and schools, charging they were victims of discrimination and protesting the failure of the U.S. education system to meet their educational needs (Gomez-Quiñones 1978; Muñoz 1989). Students cited several discriminatory practices: prohibiting the use of Spanish on school grounds, the disproportionate placement of Mexican American children in classes for the educable mentally retarded (EMR), the absence of English language programs for Spanish-speaking students, and the lack of courses on Mexican Americans (U.S. Commission on Civil Rights 1972).

Language and cultural discrimination

Discriminatory practices based on language and cultural differences were curtailed somewhat by the U.S. Department of Health, Education, and Welfare (HEW) in 1970, when it called for steps to rectify "language deficiencies" and an end to placement in EMR classes on the basis of skills in the English language. In 1970, funds were appropriated under Title VII of the Elementary and Secondary Education Act of 1968 for the development and implementation of bilingual education programs targeting low-income children with limited skill in speaking English (Grant and Goldsmith 1979; Leibowitz 1980; Plastino 1979). And as a result of several legal suits against school districts, new guidelines for placement in EMR classes were established requiring parental approval (California Advisory Committee 1977).

For higher education, change was the result of the direct action taken by Chicano students and faculty, progressive legislation, and progressive institutional policies (Muñoz 1989).

Having been the source of much of the criticism of social injustice, institutions of higher learning themselves became the targets of intense pressure by Chicanos and Chicanas (Lopez, Madrid-Barela, and Macias 1976). Institutional responses included establishing criteria that would allow institutions to give special consideration to applicants of racial and ethnic minorities and thereby provide increased access through special admissions programs.

The Civil Rights Act of 1964 prohibited discrimination on the basis of race, color, religion, or national origin in voting rights, places of public accommodations, and employment. It also established procedures whereby authorities would consider grievances, extended the life of the Commission on Civil Rights, established the Equal Employment Opportunity Commission to investigate discriminatory employment practices and the Community Relations Service to help resolve community disputes alleging discrimination, and empowered the Department of Justice to undertake legal proceedings to bring about social improvement. In this context of social and institutional change, affirmative action emerged as a controversial mechanism for social change.

Affirmative action
Affirmative action, as a means of undoing past wrongs, is rooted in the National Labor Relations Act of 1935, where it described an employer's duty to undo past wrongs against union organizers and members by rehiring workers terminated for union activity and by establishing fair policies relative to workers and free elections. In 1961, President John F. Kennedy issued Executive Order No. 10925, calling for employers to "take affirmative action to ensure that applicants are employed, and that employees are treated during employment, without regard to their race, creed, color, or national origin" (quoted in Sowell 1980, p. 1311). This executive order called for employers receiving federal contracts to ensure equality of opportunity through affirmative action.

This policy was reaffirmed in 1965 by President Lyndon B. Johnson, whose Executive Order No. 11375 required employers receiving federal government contracts greater than $10,000 to practice affirmative action. The Office of Federal Contract Compliance (OFCC) was established within the Department of Labor in 1966 to monitor the specifications of President Johnson's order. The OFCC delegated its authority to several other federal agencies, and in 1969 HEW initiated a review of affirmative action compliance by the City University of New York. In 1972, HEW issued its Higher Education Guidelines to presidents of affected colleges and universities throughout the country.

The guidelines called for written affirmative action policy, dissemination of institutional policies, appointment of Equal Employment Opportunity officers, collection and analysis of data relating to women and racial and ethnic minorities, development of mechanisms to correct deficiencies, and submission of annual reports to the Office for Civil Rights in HEW. As affirmative action practices became institutionalized in areas of employment, colleges and universities increasingly applied the notion to students, giving rise to student affirmative action programs that gave students of racial and ethnic minorities preferential treatment in admission to a limited number of slots.

Marco De Funis, a student at the University of Washington Law School, and Allan Bakke, a student at the University of California–Davis, challenged these practices, however, through legal suits in 1971 and 1974, respectively (Eastland and Bennett 1979; Livingston 1979). Both plaintiffs charged reverse discrimination when the universities rejected them while at the same time admitting racial and ethnic minority applicants with lower qualifications. The U.S. Supreme Court dismissed the *De Funis* case in 1974 on the grounds that the issue was moot because De Funis, who had been admitted pending final resolution of the case, was about to be graduated. In 1978 in the *Bakke* case, however, the U.S. Supreme Court declared that quotas are unconstitutional and ordered that Bakke be admitted. At the same time, the Court ruled that admissions programs that take race into account are acceptable. The debate over affirmative action and reverse discrimination continues to rage in the 1990s.

The collective struggle for equality receded in influence as economic recession and international issues took center stage.

Institutions' response

California took the lead among states in 1974, when the California legislature passed Assembly Concurrent Resolution (ACR) 151, calling upon institutions of higher education to prepare and implement plans that would address and overcome "ethnic, economic, and sexual underrepresentation in the makeup of the student bodies of institutions of public higher education as compared to the general ethnic, economic, and sexual composition of recent California high school graduates" (quoted in California State University and Colleges 1978, p. 1). Over the years, other states have also contended with the problematic relationship between institutions of higher education and ethnic minority groups.

Once admitted, minority students presented new problems in retention for the institutions, and academic and student support services were forced to adjust to the demands generated by the educational needs of the "new" students. Many institutions implemented specific programs designed to address the problems faced by minority college students. Like that for admissions, however, the trend to establish programs addressing minority students' needs had begun to decline by the close of the 1970s under the impact of reverse discrimination. Through most of the 1980s, under President Reagan, the needs of Chicanos and other oppressed groups declined in priority and funding. The collective struggle for equality receded in influence as economic recession and international issues took center stage.

Chicano models for educational access

Chicano models for academic success in colleges and universities stem from *El Plan de Santa Barbara* (Chicano Coordinating Council 1969). Three principles guide the model presented in that document:

1. The number of qualified Chicano students should determine the allocation of funds to programs instead of funds' determining the number of Chicano students enrolled, or *adequate funding.*
2. Colleges and universities should include Chicanos in rates that correspond to their proportion of the population within a specific geographical area, or *proportional representation.*
3. Programmatic efforts to recruit and retain Chicano students and faculty must be driven and controlled by Chicano students, administrators, employees, faculty, and community people, or *Chicano self-determination.*

The language in *El Plan de Santa Barbara* describing the relationship between Chicanos and institutions of higher learning resonates with the spirit of affirmative action as framed within the National Labor Relations Act and Executive Orders 10925 and 11375.

*Given the traditional and systemic indifference, even hos-
tility, of higher education to Chicanos, institutions must
never assume that Chicanos must first seek them out* (Chicano Coordinating Council 1969, p. 26).

The plan suggests a proactive position on the part of the institution, but one that places the program in the hands of Chicanos themselves. Combined with the principles of adequate
funding and proportional representation, this position places
responsibility on institutions of higher learning to provide
Chicanos with funds and resources to operate programs targeting Chicano students for recruitment, retention, and program completion to increase their level of educational
achievement.

A continuing struggle

Despite some initial gains in the early 1970s, Chicanos, nearly
25 years later, continue to face funding problems, are severely
underrepresented (although less so at some community colleges in the Southwest), and continue to struggle for authority
and control of Chicano-related programs. Over the years, new
plans for improving the status of Chicanos in higher education
have been developed. In 1984, for example, the Arizona Association of Chicanos for Higher Education (AACHE) put forth
its *Action Plan for Chicano Higher Education in Arizona*. The
difference between it and the Santa Barbara plan is that the
Santa Barbara plan addresses Chicanos and the Arizona plan
addresses state government units and institutions, including
colleges and universities.

Like many other Chicano higher education plans of the
1980s, the Arizona plan assesses the status of Chicanos and
other minorities at colleges and universities in that state. Central to the view presented in the plan was the notion that rapidly changing demographics requires quick adjustment on
the part of institutions to provide appropriate postsecondary
education to ethnic minorities. The Arizona plan includes
institutional plans for six colleges and universities, which
identify problems in the areas of research, faculty recruitment
and retention, student recruitment, program and curriculum
development, and community involvement. The plan also
includes specific recommendations for improvements in
each area.

Chicanos in other states also continued to press for increased access and support programs to improve their educational attainment. The Colorado Association of Chicanos in Higher Education, for instance, in its conference report *The Challenge of the Future* (1983) pointed to problems in recruitment and retention, curricula, financial aid, and representation for Chicanos on governing boards of institutions of higher learning. Within the University of Colorado, the Faculty Senate's Minority Affairs Committee (1987) also pointed to problems in these areas, calling for the establishment of an office of Dean of Minority Affairs at each of the university's campuses as a means of bringing greater coherence to the various programs addressing the educational problems faced by minority students. During the early part of the 1980s, Chicanos and other minority groups at some institutions of higher learning attempted to extend the institutional power of minority-related programs by seeking deanships of minority affairs. Institutional leadership, however, has been very reluctant to share this type of power with ethnic minorities.

Student Affirmative Action

"Student affirmative action" is rooted in the responses of California colleges and universities to the demands that racial and ethnic minorities be represented proportionally in the ranks of students. Efforts in the 1870s by the University of California to enroll Mexican American students as a means of augmenting the student body were short-lived (Leon and McNeill 1985). It was not until the turmoil of the 1960s that colleges and universities in California and throughout the country began to implement programs that targeted Chicanos for enrollment on the basis that the ethnic group was underrepresented. Informal practices began in the early 1960s, as some institutions led the pace. The University of California, for example, established its Educational Opportunity Program in 1964, later supplementing it with the Student Affirmative Action Program (University of California 1985). By academic year 1967–68, for example, five out of 19 California state institutions of higher education had established programs to provide educational opportunities for minorities (California State University and Colleges 1978). One year later, all but one of the state campuses had such programs. The California legislature recognized these educational opportunity programs in 1969, although the governor subsequently vetoed the bill recognizing it. Nonetheless, state institutions continued the programs through the internal reallocation of resources.

By the mid-1970s, over 40,000 "disadvantaged students" had been enrolled through educational opportunity programs operating at the various California institutions, which provided:

> ... support services as well as special admission to disad-
> vantaged students to assist them to function successfully
> in the collegiate environment. Each program [offered]
> recruitment and college advising, summer programs, admis-
> sions assistance, financial aid, and academic support ser
> vices, including diagnostic testing, orientation, tutoring,
> study skills, and writing and mathematics labs. Personal
> and career counseling [were] also available (California
> State University and Colleges 1978, p. 14).

At the University of California, student affirmative action "[consisted] of several interrelated programs working with targeted students from junior high school through the under-graduate years" (University of California 1985, p. 24). The programs included the Immediate Outreach Program, the Partnership Program, academic support services for university undergraduates, University Partners, and the Academic Enrichment Program. These and other similar programs, although greatly affected by fiscal and ideological problems throughout the 1980s, have provided excellent models for other colleges and universities throughout the country. It is through these programs that thousands of Chicano students have been recruited into and retained at institutions of higher education.

Entrance requirements and access

The debate surrounding the admission of racial and ethnic minorities centers on the relevance of admission criteria used by institutions of higher learning. In the Santa Barbara plan, Chicanos call for the use of culturally relevant criteria when considering Chicanos and Chicanas for admission to colleges and universities, seeing such tests and indicators as necessary to accurately assess the potential of Chicano students. Further, Chicanos call for the use of broader criteria when evaluating applicants, including evaluating recommendations from non-traditional sources (other than teachers, counselors, and so on) and conducting personal interviews to establish a subjective sense of the applicant's motivation, ability, and background. And Chicanos say that Chicanos themselves should decide about Chicano applicants, because "only people that relate to and understand the background of the Chicano student can satisfactorily make such a subjective interpretation" (Chicano Coordinating Council 1969, p. 27). Since the 1960s, Chicano applicants not meeting regular admission criteria for California higher education institutions "have been screened on the basis of one or more subjective alternative admission criteria in addition to grades and test scores" (California State University and Colleges 1978, p. 27).

Many of the reports stemming from Chicano and minority organizations continue to criticize standardized tests and other traditional criteria as the bases for admitting Chicano students to colleges and universities. In 1987, the Minority Affairs Committee of the Faculty Senate at the University of Colorado recommended that traditional admission criteria be reviewed critically and that greater emphasis be placed on "a broader range of information about the students."

Issues of access are related not only to admissions but also to recruitment practices of institutions and their sociocultural climates, including the lack of sufficient Chicano faculty and staff. Despite the implementation of aggressive recruitment programs, including precollegiate and financial aid programs, rapid growth in the number of Chicano students in universities peaked in the mid-1970s, although their enrollment rates have increased slowly since then. In the 1980s, recessions and economic woes throughout the country began to affect the budgets of colleges and universities, with monies allocated to minority-related programs decreasing. As institutions of higher learning attempted to deal with financial problems, minority-related programs frequently became targeted for cuts.

Financial assistance and access

Socioeconomic status is a factor that is highly correlated with college admission. Because Chicanos as a group are concentrated in lower socioeconomic positions, they frequently need financial assistance to enroll in college, especially as the costs of a college education have soared during the past two decades. Indeed, young Chicanos and Chicanas today might feel that they cannot possibly afford a college education and consequently not prepare themselves academically to take advantage of available opportunities.

Beginning with the National Defense Education Act (NDEA) of 1958, sometimes seen as the country's response to *Sputnik,* federal aid to students increased opportunities for college enrollment. Despite the rhetoric of "defense" and "national security," the act was the nation's first major educational measure. It provided financial aid to both institutions of higher education and college students. Grants-in-aid were made available to state schools, and graduate fellowships and student loans were made available to college students. These programs provided financial support to many minority students for the first time in U.S. history.

Five years later, the Higher Education Act of 1963 provided for the expansion of college facilities to meet increasing demands. Two years later, two immensely important federal acts relating to education were passed: the Elementary and Secondary Education Act of 1965 and the Higher Education Act of 1965. The former provided federal aid to school districts with sizable enrollments of children from low-income families, and the latter provided, among other things, federal aid to students through fellowships, scholarships, work-study programs, and guaranteed low-interest loans (Lang and Ford 1990).

The Higher Education Act of 1965 and its numerous amendments over the years have provided for a multitude of programs, including Operation Success Special Services Program, Talent Search, Upward Bound, Basic Education Opportunity Grants (later called Pell Grants), Perkins Loan Program, State Student Incentive Grant Program, Guaranteed Student Loan Program (also known as the Stafford Loan Program), Supplemental Educational Opportunity Grant Program, College Work-Study Program, and Parent Loans for Undergraduate Students Program. These programs were intended to increase college opportunities for economically disadvantaged and middle-class students. In addition, numerous other agencies began to provide financial support to minority college students, including the Ford Foundation, PEW Foundation, National Institute for Mental Health, and National Hispanic Scholarship Fund.

During the 1980s, however, many of the federally funded programs targeting members of protected classes for services and assistance came under attack by the Reagan and Bush administrations (Jackson 1990; St. John and Noell 1989). The Reagan administration, for instance, is remembered for its cut, slash, and trim approach to federal spending. Under the ideology of "reducing the deficit" and "balancing the budget," it repeatedly recommended to Congress to cut student aid programs and spending on higher education. Although Congress did not always agree, federal spending for student aid and higher education decreased considerably as a percentage of total federal outlays during the 1980s.

By the 1990s, the federal financial aid complex of the 1960s and 1970s targeting disadvantaged students had been substantially unraveled. Social security student benefits were phased out, institutions with high default rates on student loans (often historically black colleges and institutions with high concentrations of Chicanos) were removed from the Stafford Loan Program, and federal monies were shifted from student aid to research and development. Today, financial need continues to serve as a major barrier for Chicanos and Chicanas seeking a college education, and the problem is exacerbated as institutions raise their fees and tuitions to offset inflationary costs and reductions in state funding. Perhaps the greatest barriers to financial aid programs for Chicano students are their embeddedness in an ideological struggle over achievement and equity (Olivas 1984) and major problems in the distribution of funds.

Social and academic support services and access

The framers of the Santa Barbara plan saw support programs as crucial for increasing educational gains among Chicanos and Chicanas. Support programs would establish "a stable academic, political, and financial base for Chicano students" (Chicano Coordinating Council 1969, p. 32). In contrast, remedial and compensatory programs would "alter the student[s] to conform to a prescribed norm of academic and social behavior" (p. 32) rather than provide relevant educational experiences. Such support programs would require the development of new structures and processes not found at institutions of higher education. Chicano student organizations were given the task of ensuring that support programs provided services that were directly relevant to the educational needs of Chicano students.

The Santa Barbara plan recommended orientation programs that would address issues of cultural identity, provide academic support, and encourage achievement. It noted that student support programs—counseling, tutoring, legal, health, housing, transportation, library, financial, and career counseling services—needed to change to be more relevant to the needs of Chicano students. Rather than changing Chicano students to function in an "American" college setting, U.S. colleges and universities needed to change to meet the educational needs of Chicano students. The premise underlying the view in the Santa Barbara plan is that the larger society and its institutions had imposed a negative self-image on Chicanos, who, despite their ability to perform well in college, needed strong reinforcement and encouragement.

Colleges and universities responded by establishing an array of student support programs. Numerous precollegiate, summer bridge, orientation, academic support, and social support organizations were developed and implemented. They varied in terms of institutions' financial support, the degree of control Chicanos and Chicanas had in the operation of the programs, and their relative permanence. California tended to lead the country in the recruitment and retention of Chicanos at its colleges and universities, and the University of California, in particular, was very aggressive. Others, like the University of Colorado, lagged by several years in many programs. It was not until the late 1980s, for instance, that precollegiate programs were established at Colorado campuses. In all, many Chicano students benefited from the services offered by the programs at many colleges and universities.

Despite numerous gains in educational attainment among Chicano college students during the 1970s, however, achievement tended to remain low, with the percentage of Chicano students receiving postsecondary degrees remaining in the single digits to the present. The attacks on programs for minorities throughout the country during the 1980s created a crisis in the relationship between Chicanos and institutions of higher learning. The high dropout rate among Chicano high school students exacerbated the situation, as did the nativistic movements among "Americans." The rise of conservatism during the 1980s produced a strategy of political correctness that continues to challenge multiculturalism, bilingual education, and pluralist values.

The Development of Chicano Studies

Units in Chicano studies range from academic programs to departments to research centers (Martinez 1990). Chicano studies were first established at U.S. colleges and universities during the late 1960s as a direct result of the struggles of Chicano students, faculty, and community members (Muñoz 1989; Sanchez 1974). The units have experienced both calm and turbulent times, enjoying periods of significant interest from students and surviving fiscally induced institutional reorganizations. Over the past quarter century, units in Chicano studies have promoted the enrollment of Chicano students, developed and made available Chicano-based curricula, provided research and publishing support to faculty members and students, and served as a nexus for communications of Chicano-related activities.

Chicano studies, as envisioned by Chicano supporters, would bring the knowledge of the Ivory Tower to bear on the problems facing Chicano communities. Chicano studies would contribute to the liberation of Chicano *barrios* and *pueblos* by providing resources for collective self-reflection and problem solving. Instead, over the years they have been forced to wrestle with problems of legitimacy, autonomy, financial resources, and intragroup conflict, and they have yet to establish the relationship with Chicano communities that once inspired them. Still, they have provided the first significant group of Chicano and Chicana scholars in the history of the ethnic group. Collective self-reflection has yielded many new theoretical avenues by which to study Chicanos as a distinct ethnic group, one with its own sources of cultural energy and history.

Philosophical and social objectives

The principal view underlying the establishment of Chicano studies programs in colleges and universities held that these institutions can be sources of major change in society. Indeed, the universities were seen as latent agents of change whose resources, especially knowledge, could be used to transform the socioeconomic conditions oppressing Chicano communities. The liberation of Chicano communities from Anglo-American society was the cornerstone of the ideology of Chicano studies. This pragmatic view of institutions of higher learning guided the establishment of most Chicano studies programs in the late 1960s, and institutions responded by establishing an array of structural units with more or less power and autonomy.

The intellectual direction for Chicano studies came from the work of Don Octavio Romano and his students at the University of California–Berkeley. Through *El Grito: The Journal of Mexican American Thought,* Romano and his students broke the intellectual hegemony that Anglo-American scholars held on the study and portrayal of Mexican Americans. Romano and other intellectuals of his day argued that social science was politically linked to an ideology of oppression that espoused assimilation and acculturation (Martinez 1990). The social science literature before the development of Chicano studies supported racist stereotypes of Mexican Americans as ahistorical, fatalistic beings who must adopt Anglo-American cultural practices. It was Chicano studies that began with the assumption that Chicanos were active, creative beings with a common culture and collective consciousness who were forced to survive hostile social conditions. In their struggle, Chicanos generate the historical process, create and re-create forms of community, and generate collective experiences that serve as guideposts in the struggle against adversity.

The liberation of Chicano communities from Anglo-American society was the cornerstone of the ideology of Chicano studies.

NACS
The founders of the National Association for Chicano Studies (NACS), the official professional association for Chicano studies, held the same viewpoint. Established in 1973, the organization holds annual conferences that bring Chicano and Chicana scholars from throughout the country to present results of research and studies on Chicano communities. The organization also serves as a valuable mechanism of socialization for students who attend the conference and participate every year. Many Chicano graduate students present their first professional paper at the NACS conference, while others make their first professional presentations.

Change in the curricula
The establishment of Chicano studies as interdisciplinary academic units resulted in the development of many new courses on Chicanos and Chicanas. The roots of these units, however, are found in the first set of courses offered at Anglo-American colleges and universities. The first Chicano studies courses were offered at California colleges and universities in fall 1968, and, by the early 1970s, many colleges and universities throughout the Southwest and the Midwest had established Chicano studies programs and regularly offered courses in Chicano studies.

By the time *El Plan de Santa Barbara* was presented in 1969, courses on Chicanos and Mexican Americans had already been taught at many institutions, especially in California. The plan contained program and course models, arguing that Chicano studies could be most effective as departments. The curriculum offered through such departments would "take into account the Chicano student's especial psychological, social, and intellectual needs" (Chicano Coordinating Council 1969, p. 44). Chicano studies curricula would contain lower- and upper-division courses, elaborated in accordance with faculty appointments. The curriculum would be organized into three broad areas of study: humanities, social sciences, and education. Core requirements would include disciplines within each area, and, at the lower division, culture and communications would be emphasized to affirm identity and to develop a deep appreciation for cultural heritage. Upper-division curricula would be organized around required survey courses from history, economics, psychology, sociology, literature and folklore, politics, and education. The curricula had (and continue to have) two aims: (1) to provide a socially relevant education that prepares Chicano students to serve the needs of Chicano communities, and (2) to develop an increased appreciation for cultural heritage among all students, thereby enriching the total society.

The integration of Chicano studies programs and centers within institutions of higher education, however, has been marginal. In 1993, students at the University of California–Los Angeles marched, rallied, and fasted in an effort to have Chicano studies upgraded to departmental status (Rodriguez 1993). The result was an agreement to establish the Cesar Chavez Center for Interdisciplinary Instruction in Chicana and Chicano Studies as part of a broader array of centers for interdisciplinary instruction (UCLA News 1993). While the outcome seems to ensure the stability of Chicana and Chicano studies at UCLA, it is a compromise that maintains Chicanos and Chicanas in marginal positions with regard to academic departments.

Students' achievement
Educational achievement among Chicanos must be understood historically and statistically; that is, the changes that occurred during the 1960s in the relationship between Chicanos and institutions of higher education have both a political and a numerical significance. First, as a result of the educational opportunities made available to racial and ethnic

minorities in this country in the 1960s, the first significant number of Chicano intellectuals came into existence. Chicano students, for the first time, were afforded opportunities for graduate education that culminated in doctoral or professional degrees.

Chicanos, the "forgotten people," have never had federally supported colleges and universities dedicated to their education and intellectual growth. During the 1940s and 1950s, the number of Mexican American scholars was quite small, and when colleges and universities began demanding them, there were not enough to fill the positions created by the Chicano student movement. The gap created many opportunities for teaching, research, and administration for Chicanos and Chicanas without doctoral degrees in hand. They were, however, the persons most informed about the needs and problems of the Chicano community and the most able to develop relevant curricula, research projects, and support programs.

Statistically, Chicano students' achievement improved both absolutely and relatively. In the 1960s, Chicano youth began to attend colleges and universities in substantially greater numbers. Between 1968 and 1972, the number of students with Spanish surnames enrolled in colleges and universities increased from 49,205 to 130,840, from 1.7 percent of the undergraduate student population to 2.4 percent (Lopez, Madrid Barela, and Macias 1976). While the relative growth might not appear substantial—and the number of Chicanos and other minorities enrolled in institutions of higher education remains depressingly low—the absolute growth in the number of Chicano students produced a qualitative change in the intellectual environment for Chicanos. Indeed, it produced an intellectual environment, a community of Chicano intellectuals.

This intelligentsia administered Chicano studies programs and departments, offered Chicano-centered curricula, and promoted a sociocultural climate on campus that helped Chicano students survive the rigors of higher education. Chicano studies influenced thousands of Chicano students in their understanding of history and their ethnic consciousness, while offering non-Chicano students opportunities to learn about themselves through different cultural viewpoints. Overall, Chicanos' educational achievement in colleges and universities is reflected in increased numbers of participants at every level of higher education, although numbers have not increased qualitatively since the late 1960s and early 1970s. Today, Chicanos continue to be underrepresented at institutions of higher education relative to their proportion in the overall population.

Summary

Access to institutions of higher education has improved slowly for Chicanos and other minorities. During the 1960s, as a result of widespread racial unrest, the federal government took important steps in the form of legislation and policies to provide educational opportunity to oppressed and disadvantaged groups in this country. Chicano students, faculty, and community members brought to light the problematic relationship between Chicanos and institutions of higher education. Institutional responses included an array of student recruitment and retention programs, affirmative action plans for staff and faculty, and Chicano studies programs. The responses produced significant results in the short term, with thousands of Chicanos and Chicanas enrolling in colleges and universities throughout the country, primarily in the Southwest. From these groups of students emerged the first significant number of Chicano intellectuals, an intelligentsia that embarked on the study of Chicano communities to understand their social problems and provide direction for their resolution.

Despite the initial gains in Chicano students' achievement, educators and policy makers expressed serious concerns in the early 1980s about the underrepresentation of Chicanos in higher education. Chicanos have made many recommendations over the last decade for increasing the number of Chicanos and Chicanas among undergraduate and graduate ranks. Some institutions have responded to the crisis of the 1980s in ethnic minorities' education by strengthening their commitments and contributions to equal opportunities for higher education. California's legislature, Department of Education, and systems of postsecondary education have led the country in responding to the educational needs of Chicano students. The fiscal crisis in California today, however, bodes ill for the educational future of Chicanos. Perhaps institutions in other states will move to share the responsibility of providing equal educational opportunity for Chicanos.

THE PARTICIPATION OF CHICANOS IN HIGHER EDUCATION

The participation of Chicano students in institutions of higher education began in the middle of the 19th century. Although some wealthy Mexican families have sent their children to study at U.S. colleges and universities, over the years most Mexican American and Chicano youth have remained outside the arena of higher education, excluded by ethnocentric, racist, and sexist conceptions of higher education and by selective admissions criteria. The Servicemen's Readjustment Act of 1944, the G.I. Bill of Rights, provided federal aid in the areas of education, hospitalization, loan applications, and other benefits to veterans of World War II, which were later extended to veterans of the Korean and Vietnam conflicts. Along with the assistance and protection provided by the National Defense and Education Act of 1958, the Civil Rights Act of 1964, and the Higher Education Act of 1965, these benefits were the initial bridges that brought Chicanos and Chicanas into institutions of higher learning in relatively substantial numbers.

Only since the 1960s have data on Chicanos and other Hispanic populations been systematically collected; before then, such data were virtually nonexistent. Although limited to a 5 percent sample, the 1970 Census was the first to include a fixed-choice opportunity to designate oneself as of Spanish origin, making it possible to develop socioeconomic profiles of Chicano communities. The 1980 Census used the question of Spanish origin or descent on all questionnaires, and the 1990 Census included a refined version of the question on all of its questionnaires. As a result, the data are not directly comparable across the points of collection, especially the 1970 data, but they are nonetheless extremely valuable in providing information about Chicanos, including Mexican and Mexican American citizens (de la Puente 1992).

This section reviews enrollment trends among Chicano students in postsecondary education, examining patterns of enrollment in two-year and in four-year and graduate institutions; reviewing college completion rates, the pipelines to graduate schools, graduate enrollments, and patterns of completion; and discussing the general implications of the trends characterizing the relationship between Chicanos and Chicanas and the U.S. system of higher education.

The Undergraduate Experience
Ancient Greek educators, despite being sexist and elitist, held

a view of education that has undergirded European and U.S. perspectives on the mission and purpose of higher education. The ancient Greeks saw education (culture) as the path to a good and healthy life and to increased understanding (knowledge) of ourselves as human beings. Education was to prepare individuals to become immersed in the civic affairs and artistic creations of society, and to engage them in contemplating the highest ideas and ideals. From this view, education is seen as a force in the pursuit of a healthy and moral life. American undergraduate colleges and universities are modeled on English universities, which are rooted in this view of education. To be sure, these institutions have experienced many changes since the 17th century, when they were first established in this country (Smith 1990).

The early colleges
The first colleges in the United States were private and offered curricula couched in theological frameworks. Early state universities founded during the early part of the 1800s tended to reaffirm a medieval course of study. Agriculture, engineering, and other technical areas were not included as part of the curriculum until the establishment of land-grant colleges following passage of the Morrill Act in 1862. Land-grant colleges gave rise to a boom of professional academicians who quickly began to transform the curriculum by introducing new disciplines and subjects, promoting notions of "electives" and "academic freedom," and establishing departments as the basic academic units within colleges and universities. This generation of professional academicians abandoned, to a great extent, traditional authority, replacing it with rational-legal, or bureaucratic, authority.

As institutions of higher education continued to change, liberal education increasingly became regarded as a limited component of an undergraduate education. Over time these institutions became more and more focused on practical training and research, especially as graduate schools were established. In the early 20th century, some institutions (such as Columbia University and Antioch) experimented with course concentrations and distributions, general education requirements, and comprehensive examinations as ways of bringing cohesion to the undergraduate experience (Smith 1990). Over time, general education supplanted liberal education, except at small, denominational, liberal arts colleges.

Post-World War II

In the years following World War II, the U.S. system of higher education entered a period of prolonged growth (1945 to 1985), with the number of colleges and universities more than doubling and enrollments more than quadrupling. Bachelor's degrees more than tripled as more and more persons entered and completed college programs. Only recently have colleges and universities experienced severe fiscal problems that have required cutting back staff, faculty, and other personnel.

Chicano students entered the U.S. system of education in relatively substantial numbers during the 1960s, although slight increases also occurred in the 1950s as a result of the G.I. Bill of Rights and increased opportunities for an undergraduate education at community colleges. The system they found was one that reflected all of the changes that had taken place since the 17th century: It was bureaucratic in nature, run by professional academicians with links to societal centers of power, focused on general education and training in liberal education, and completely oblivious to the educational needs of Chicano and Chicana students.

In general, the U.S. undergraduate experience takes place at four-year institutions, although many students begin their postsecondary education at two-year institutions. Over the past two decades, the majority of undergraduate students (approximately 62.5 percent) have been enrolled at four-year institutions. Unlike Anglo-Americans, however, the typical Chicano undergraduate does not begin at a four-year institution, but at a two-year college.

Enrollment at Community Colleges

The establishment of a junior college at the University of Chicago early in the 1890s reflected the continued expansion and differentiation of the U.S. system of higher education. The purpose of the junior college was to prepare students to transfer to the senior college. Soon after, other private colleges established junior colleges, and the first Associate of Arts degree was awarded in 1900 at the University of Chicago. In the public sector, the first junior or community college was founded in Joliet, Illinois, in 1901. A few years later, in 1907, California established its first public two-year college. By 1915, more than 70 community and junior colleges existed throughout the country—by 1930, more than 200. By the early 1970s, more than 1,100 community colleges had been established in the United States, the overwhelming majority of them public institutions (Olivas 1979).

Community and junior colleges generally follow liberal admissions policies, charge nominal or no fees and tuition, and offer both academic and vocational curricula. The community college graduate ordinarily earns an associate degree, especially an Associate of Arts. These colleges have pioneered in offering courses during evening and weekend hours, part-time study programs, and other services to their communities.

Patterns of enrollment

In 1970, nearly four of every five (77.8 percent) white undergraduates were enrolled in four-year colleges and universities (Lopez, Madrid-Barela, and Macias 1976). Ten years later, approximately three of every four (76.9 percent) white undergraduates enrolled in institutions of higher education were at four-year institutions (National Center for Education Statistics 1992b). By 1990, the proportion had dropped to approximately two of every three (63.3 percent) white undergraduates enrolled at four-year institutions, and by fall 1991, the ratio had increased to nearly three out of four (71.4 percent) (Evangelauf 1993). In contrast, Hispanic undergraduates were more likely than their white counterparts to be enrolled at community or junior colleges. In 1970, nearly half (45 percent) of Hispanic undergraduates were enrolled in community and junior colleges (Lopez, Madrid-Barela, and Macias 1976). By 1980, this pattern had strengthened, with slightly more than half (54 percent) of Hispanic undergraduates enrolled at two-year institutions (National Center for Education Statistics 1992b), and by fall 1991, the percentage had increased to 60.1 percent (Evangelauf 1993). As a result, Hispanic undergraduates are concentrated in community colleges relative to their white counterparts.

Data including the variable of gender are available for 1975, although they are not available by institutional levels. In 1975, approximately 411,000 Hispanics were enrolled in institutions of higher education. Of those students, 192,000 (46.7 percent) were females, while, among whites, 43.9 percent were women. By 1985, the number of Hispanic undergraduate students enrolled at colleges and universities in this country had risen to approximately 579,000, 299,000 (51.6 percent) of them female. Women accounted for 50 percent of white undergraduate enrollments that same year. In 1990, approximately 617,000 Hispanic undergraduates attended institutions of higher learning, 321,000 (52 percent) of them women. Similarly, females accounted for 51.7 percent of the white student population.

Overall, Chicanos and other minority groups are more likely to attend community and junior colleges than members of the dominant group. Ironically, public two-year colleges have provided less financial aid to students than have four-year colleges and universities and depend more on federal funding than the other institutions (Olivas 1981). As a result, Chicano students, as a group, receive less financial aid than their counterparts in the dominant group, relatively speaking, and could be disproportionately affected by cutbacks in federal support to community colleges.

The transfer dilemma for Chicanos

Transfer from a community college to a four-year institution is crucial to increasing educational achievement among Chicanos, because two-year institutions are the educational contexts in which Chicanos and other Hispanic undergraduates are concentrated. Community colleges are the pipelines carrying students to higher levels of the educational system. How well they perform this function, however, has been a subject of considerable concern and debate.

Community colleges are part of the expansion and differentiation of the U.S. system of higher education (Karabel 1972). Stressing their open and democratic character, these institutions are part of an overall stratified system of higher education that "distributes people in a manner [that] is roughly commensurate with both their class origins and their occupational destiny" (p. 525). Moreover, by the early 1970s, just as enrollments of ethnic minorities were increasing, community colleges were moving toward emphasizing vocational rather than transfer curricula, thereby channeling these first-generation college students into terminal, blue-collar programs.

The turn toward vocational programs directly contributed to the decline in transfer rates among community colleges. In the early 1980s, however, the transfer rate of students completing the requirements for academic Associate of Arts degrees also declined (Grubb 1991). Analyses of data from longitudinal studies, including the National Longitudinal Study of the Class of 1972 and the High School and Beyond Study of the high school class of 1980, indicate that the transfer rate was higher among the members of the class of 1972 (28.7 percent) than among the class of 1980 (20.2 percent) (Grubb 1991). Among Hispanics, the rates were 25.9 percent and 15.7 percent, respectively. (Readers should note that most studies of community colleges have focused on specific institutions.)

Institutional features

Studies of community colleges located in the borderland areas of Texas, Arizona, and California have shown that Hispanic students (mostly Chicanos) have a desire to transfer but that several social and institutional factors mitigate their doing so (Rendon, Justiz, and Resta 1988). Social factors like poverty and unemployment set limits on changing residences and paying educational costs. Indeed, socioeconomic status is one of the factors most strongly related to educational achievement in general (Bender 1991). Faculty, counselors, and other personnel tend not to encourage transfers.

Many scholars emphasize the need to create conditions that promote the social integration of minority students within the culture and practices of colleges (Pincus and DeCamp 1989). Doing so would improve the retention of minority students and prevent the already small pools of potential minority transferees from decreasing. How might minority students be integrated within community colleges? Longitudinal studies show that students who transfer might be aided by housing and work-study opportunities at the four-year institution (Nora and Horvath 1989; Velez and Javalgi 1987). In addition, collaboration between two-year and four-year institutions is an important institutional response in addressing problems in the transfer process (Sotello and Turner 1992). During the late 1980s, many institutions developed forms of collaboration to increase the transfer rate among students, including "articulation agreements" that were intended to facilitate the transfer process (Barkley 1993). If these approaches work—and one wonders just how many resources institutional leaders are willing to commit to the process of transferring—the problem of bringing those students who transfer to completion of a bachelor's degree remains to be addressed by the four-year institutions.

The structural dilemma facing Chicanos and Chicanas with regard to community colleges is that while these institutions are more accessible (both economically and academically) than four-year institutions, structurally they fulfill distributive functions within a stratification system that channels people into statuses on the basis of class, race, and gender. Were Chicano and Chicana students aware of this structural dilemma, it would behoove them, from the perspective of rational choice, to apply to a four-year institution at the outset of their postsecondary education. But other factors mitigate the information they have about these choices, and economic hardships continue to set constraints on them.

Enrollment and Completions at Four-Year Colleges

Four-year institutions include universities with graduate programs and professional schools. In 1970, students with Spanish surnames accounted for approximately 1.5 percent of the overall student population at four-year colleges and universities, including the private and public sectors (Lopez, Madrid-Barela, and Macias 1976). By 1980, Hispanics accounted for 1.8 percent of the student population at four-year institutions—by fall 1991, 4.4 percent of the enrollments at four-year colleges and universities (Evangelauf 1993). In absolute numbers, Hispanic enrollments at four-year colleges and universities ranged from 56,490 in 1970 to over 344,000 in 1990 and 383,000 in 1991 (Cabrera 1978; Collison 1992; Evangelauf 1993; Lopez, Madrid-Barela, and Macias 1976; National Center for Education Statistics 1992b). While Hispanics accounted for 4.5 percent of the national population in 1970, in 1990 they accounted for 9 percent and are considered among the fastest-growing ethnic groups in this country (U.S. Bureau of the Census 1991b).

Problems of students' dropping out of college continue to reduce potential completion rates among Chicano students at colleges and universities in this country. This problem is evident in the statistical gap between Chicano enrollments and the number of degrees obtained. More Chicano students enroll in institutions of higher learning than earn degrees, with the difference directly because of attrition. For example, in academic year 1986–87, Hispanics earned only 19,345 (4.4 percent) of the 436,308 associate degrees conferred in this country, yet they made up approximately 7.7 percent of the student population of two-year colleges (National Center for Education Statistics 1991a). This problem is particularly acute given that Chicanos are highly concentrated in two-year institutions.

It would behoove Chicano students to apply to a four-year institution at the outset of their postsecondary education.

The number of bachelor's degrees earned by Hispanics in 1970 is an estimated 1.5 percent of the total number of four-year degrees conferred. At the same time, Hispanics made up 1.5 percent of the undergraduate population at four-year colleges and universities (Cabrera 1978). Although greatly underrepresented at these institutions, a significant gap was not apparent between enrollment and completion rates at that time. By 1986, however, Hispanics made up 3.6 percent of the undergraduate population at four-year institutions, yet they obtained only 2.7 percent of the bachelor's degrees awarded in 1987 (Carter and Wilson 1991; National Center for Education Statistics 1992b). Of the 26,990 degrees awarded to Hispanic students, females earned 52 percent (National Center for Education Statistics 1991a). Including community college undergraduates on the basis that transfer is the objective only widens the gap between enrollments (5.3 percent) and bachelor's degrees earned (2.7 percent).

Of the 792,656 bachelor's degrees conferred in 1970, Hispanics earned an estimated 11,900 (1.5 percent); of the 1,949,657 conferred in 1990, Hispanics earned approximately 52,600 (2.7 percent). Because Mexican Americans or Chicanos accounted for approximately 60 percent of the Hispanic population in this country in 1970, Chicanos earned approximately 7,140 of the estimated 11,900 bachelor's degrees earned by Hispanics that year. All other factors being equal, Chicanos, as a distinct ethnic group, thus earned approximately 0.9 percent of the bachelor's degrees conferred in 1970. Further, of the 52,600 bachelor's degrees awarded to Hispanics in 1990, Chicanos earned an estimated 32,612 (62 percent). Chicanos, then, would have earned approximately 1.7 percent of the bachelor's degrees conferred in 1990. Estimates for 1991 indicate that of the 1,094,538 bachelor's degrees awarded, Chicanas and Chicanos earned approximately 22,699 (2.1 percent) of them (Stewart 1993). Despite increases in both absolute and relative terms, the relative proportion of Chicanos and Chicanas earning bachelor's degrees remains very low, and the group as a whole is greatly underrepresented among recipients of bachelor's degrees in this country.

Recent information from students who enrolled as freshmen at National Collegiate Athletic Association (NCAA) Division I schools in academic year 1985–86 indicate that only 54 percent graduated within six years. Only 41 percent of the Hispanic students, however, graduated within this time frame, compared to 56 percent of the white students. The completion rate for Hispanic women (44 percent) was slightly higher than for Hispanic men (39 percent), while the completion rates for white women and men were 58 percent and 55 percent, respectively (Cage 1993).

Where Do Chicanos Go after College?

Completing the requirements for a bachelor's degree brings an end to the college experience for most graduating students: The need for full-time employment and the increasing costs of a college education are probably the major factors responsible. Indeed, obtaining a bachelor's degree is a final educational objective for most graduates. Traditionally, the bachelor's degree has been the ticket that provided access to careers with prestige and income. Studies of social stratification frequently show the return from a college education in terms of occupational prestige and income. Higher education, or rather the lack of it, has relevance for oppressed groups in ways qualitatively different from occupational prestige and earnings.

The relative destruction of indigenous institutions and systemic denial of access into dominant group institutions of higher education are processes embedded in the larger process of cultural genocide. Chicanos, as an ethnic group, historically have not had the institutional space to reflect on their group identity, history, and future. Yet institutionalized practices supporting group intellectual pursuits are crucial for understanding self and group. These processes have been checked among Chicanos by institutional and ideological barriers imposed by the dominant group. And since the advent of graduate and professional degrees, access to the upper reaches of higher education has become increasingly necessary for developing a deep understanding of human and group existence and to obtain the credentials needed to gain access to graduate education.

Graduate education

During the 12th century in Europe, doctoral degrees were first awarded as honorary degrees indicating respect for a recipient's learning. During the 13th and 14th centuries, doctoral degrees were also conferred as earned degrees. Master's and doctoral degrees were synonymous and represented the most distinguished title of scholarly achievement. The doctoral degree preceded the baccalaureate degree, with the latter developing in progress to the "mastership." Graduate programs were introduced to U.S. colleges and universities in the 19th century, with many already in existence at the beginning of the 20th century.

During the 19th century, many U.S. students earned doctoral degrees in Europe, especially in Germany, where universities' admissions policies were less restrictive and academic freedom greater than in England and France. Not surprisingly, when graduate programs were established in this country, they were modeled on the graduate schools in Germany—requiring the imposition of a German institutional model (graduate school) on an English institutional model (undergraduate school).

Today, graduate education is the process that takes the student well beyond the understanding developed during the undergraduate years. In many graduate education programs, students are asked to address seriously fundamental questions about human existence and social organization; they are asked to apply the tools of their trade in the production of knowledge about the physical and social worlds. While some in society complain about "degree inflation," it is a general truth that access to graduate education and graduate schools is crucial to the development of an understanding among Chicanos and Chicanas of their contemporary existence. This understanding of one's own group ruptures the ideological hegemony of the dominant group and creates the potential for a deeper group understanding.

Where do Chicanos and Chicanas end up after college? Like other graduates, most of them end up in their chosen field or a related one; unlike their white counterparts, however, fewer of them continue their education by enrolling in graduate school. Indeed, the Mexican American intelligentsia before the 1960s was comprised of a handful of scholars and activists. It was not until the 1960s that Chicanos began enrolling in graduate and professional programs in relatively substantial numbers. The pipeline to graduate school, however, expands and contracts in accordance with political and economic dynamics that open and close doors of opportunity to Chicanos.

Graduate enrollment

The country's universities had long offered professional degrees in law and medicine by the time the first earned doc-

toral degrees were awarded in 1861. Earned master's degree
were first awarded a few years later at Harvard University
(1881–82). Although enrollments in graduate schools started
slowly, by the beginning of this century 5,668 students were
enrolled in graduate schools throughout this country, by 1950
nearly 250,000, and by the 1980s nearly 500,000. The number
of Chicanos enrolled as graduate students during the first half
of this century is unknown. A survey of graduate institutions
in the early 1970s reported that only about one-third of the
institutions in the sample regularly collected data on the ethnic and racial identification of their graduate students (Hamilton 1973). Thus, the data used to compose a portrait of Chicanos in graduate education necessarily must come from the
last three decades.

In 1970, 5,976 students with Spanish surnames were
enrolled in graduate and professional schools, accounting
for 1.2 percent of the student population (Lopez, Madrid-
Barela, and Macias 1976). By 1972, the number had increased
to 8,476, 1.4 percent of the overall student population in graduate and professional schools. During this period, students
with Spanish surnames in graduate schools (not including
professional schools) were concentrated in education, arts
and humanities, and social sciences, followed by enrollments
in business, biological sciences, engineering, and physical
sciences. In doctorate-granting institutions, students with
Spanish surnames accounted for 1.1 percent of the students
enrolled in 1973. By 1976, 8,045 Hispanics were enrolled in
graduate schools, 1.9 percent of the graduate student population. That same year, 4,104 were enrolled in professional
schools, or 1.9 percent of that student population. By 1984,
Hispanic enrollments had increased to 12,715 in graduate
schools and 8,117 in professional schools, accounting for 2.8
percent and 4.1 percent, respectively (Brown 1987).

Graduate enrollments increased for Hispanics and other
minorities between 1984 and 1986 (Wilson and Carter 1988),
to 3.2 percent of the graduate student population, the highest
point in the group's history. Between 1986 and 1988, however,
Hispanics experienced the only decline in graduate enrollments, a 15.2 percent drop or approximately 7,000 graduate
students (Carter and Wilson 1991). In 1990, 46,000 Hispanics
were enrolled in graduate education (2.9 percent of the graduate student population), and 10,000 were enrolled in professional schools (3.6 percent of the professional school pop-

ulation) (Collison 1992). A year later, 51,000 Hispanics (3.1 percent) were enrolled in graduate programs, and 11,000 (3.9 percent) were enrolled in professional schools (Evangelauf 1993).

While Hispanic enrollments in graduate and professional schools overall increased substantially in absolute terms over the past two decades (from 6,000 to 62,000), relatively speaking they have posted little gain (increasing from 1.3 percent to 3 percent) (Brown 1987; Collison 1992; Evangelauf 1993). Moreover, the proportion of low-income Hispanics enrolled in colleges and universities declined during the 1980s (Wilson and Carter 1988). Chicanas and other ethnic minority women have experienced higher enrollment gains than their male counterparts over recent years, but like the latter they remain greatly underrepresented in institutions of higher education (Casas and Ponterotto 1984; Melendez and Petrovich 1989; Vigil 1988).

Matriculation and completion

Like the situation in undergraduate education, enrollment in graduate and professional programs does not equal the number of degrees obtained. The result is a gap between matriculation and completion of the requirements for a degree. Of the 20,641 doctoral degrees awarded in 1972–73, Chicanos received 93, or 0.4 percent of the total (Lopez, Madrid-Barela, and Macias 1976). Most were in education, arts and humanities, life sciences, and engineering and physical sciences. In 1973–74, Spanish Americans earned 149 (0.7 percent) of the 22,693 doctoral degrees conferred upon U.S.-born citizens (Cabrera 1978). Yet, as noted previously, several thousand students with Spanish surnames were enrolled in graduate schools during this period.

In 1976, Hispanics earned 534 doctoral degrees, or 1.8 percent of the total conferred (Brown 1987). Although the number dropped to 452 (1.6 percent) in 1978, by 1984 the number of Hispanics who earned doctoral degrees rebounded to 616 (2.4 percent of the total). By 1989, however, these numbers had decreased to 570 (2.5 percent) of the doctoral degrees awarded to U.S. citizens (Carter and Wilson 1991). Between 1970 and 1990, the relative percentage of Chicanos (Mexican Americans) of the Hispanic population in this country increased from 60 percent to 62 percent. While the nature of the data does not permit an examination of percentages of Chicano and Chicana doctoral recipients, crude estimates would place the average number of doctoral degrees earned annually by Chicanos during the 1980s at approximately 330 (61 percent of the Hispanic population). A further estimate would place the total of doctoral degrees earned by Chicanos during the 1980s at 3,300. Estimates for 1991 indicate that of the 39,294 doctoral degrees awarded, Chicanos earned approximately 454 (1.2 percent) of the total (Stewart 1993). The pipeline to graduate education appears to be drying up quickly.

Shifting numbers

Over the last two decades, the number and relative percentage of Hispanics receiving first professional degrees (in law, medicine, dentistry, pharmacology, and business, for example) have increased slowly but steadily. The 1,079 Hispanics receiving their first professional degrees in 1976 accounted for 1.7 percent of all the first professional degrees awarded that year. By 1981, the figures had increased to 1,541 and 2.2 percent and by 1985, to 1,884 and 2.7 percent, respectively. In 1987, 2,051 Hispanics received first professional degrees, or 2.9 percent of all recipients of first professional degrees that year. And in 1989, 2,254 Hispanics earned first professional degrees, or 3.2 percent of this group's recipients (Carter and Wilson 1991). Hispanic women have made major gains in both gender and ethnic categories. Evenly underrepresented at 1.7 percent of recipients within their own gender in 1976, Hispanic women increased to 3.5 percent in 1989, while Hispanic men increased to 3 percent. Within their ethnic category, Hispanic women accounted for only 15.2 percent of Hispanic recipients of first professional degrees in 1976, increasing to 39.3 percent in 1989.

Between 1970 and 1990, approximately 6.4 million master's degrees were awarded in this country (National Center for Education Statistics 1991a). Specific figures on the numbers of Chicanos and Chicanas who earn master's degrees are few and difficult to locate, but the American Council on Education reports frequencies and percentages for 1976 at 5,299 (1.7 percent), 1981 at 6,461 (2.2 percent), 1985 at 6,864 (2.4 percent), 1987 at 7,044 (2.4 percent), and 1989 at 7,270 (2.4 percent) (Carter and Wilson 1991). Overall, while the genders were equally represented in 1976, increases among women and decreases among men resulted in slight imbalances by

1989 (2.3 percent of Hispanic men and 2.4 percent of Hispanic women) (Carter and Wilson 1991). Despite imbalances
between genders, however, estimates for 1991 indicate that
of the 337,168 master's degrees awarded, Chicanas and Chicanos earned approximately 5,197, or 1.5 percent (Stewart
1993). Thus, the number of Chicanas and Chicanos earning
master's degrees is decreasing and could continue to decrease
through the 1990s.

Trends in Enrollments and Expected Completions

Patterns indicated by aggregate data analyses and studies show
that Chicanos and other Hispanics, while increasing in terms
of enrollments in higher education and in the number of
degrees received, remain underrepresented relative to their
counterparts in the dominant group. Patterns of enrollment
and degree attainment over the past two decades show that
growth has been slow, but fairly consistent. Furthermore,
rates have increased faster among Hispanic women than
among men.

Total enrollment in postsecondary educational institutions
is expected to increase from approximately 13.9 million in
1990 to 15.7 million by 2000 (National Center for Education
Statistics 1991d). Generally, enrollments among ethnic minorities are projected to continue to increase faster than among
Anglo-Americans, with the highest rates expected among
Asian-Americans and Hispanics. (Enrollments among Hispanics increased from 472,000 in 1980 to 758,000 in 1990, an
increase of 61 percent.)

Enrollments of Hispanics are expected to increase to 1 million by 2000, which, if realized, would reflect an increase of
32 percent, rather than a projected 43 percent increase based
on 1990 enrollment estimates. Enrollments among women
in general are expected to increase at higher rates than among
men. Among Hispanics, the enrollment of women is projected
to increase by 51 percent between 1990 and 2000. In contrast,
the enrollment among Hispanic men is projected to increase
by 35 percent during the same period.

In general, trends and projections indicate that as the absolute number of Hispanic enrollments in institutions of higher
education increases, the *rate* of increase decreases. The relatively high rates of increase during the 1970s and 1980s result
from the small number of Chicanos and other Hispanics
enrolled in colleges and universities. If Hispanic enrollments

increase to 1 million by 2000, they will account for an estimated 6.4 percent of overall enrollments in higher education.

But how does enrollment relate to completion of graduate degrees? Expected patterns of completion involve evaluative components and raise ethical and moral issues regarding acceptable levels of completion rates among an oppressed ethnic minority group—issues that can quickly become too intellectually (politically) complex for developing practical solutions if one does not recognize that goals (not quotas) are necessary components of plans to improve completion rates among minority college students.

Completion rates for college students, especially ethnic minority students, are a function of the sociopolitical dynamics of the day. That is, government sponsored financial aid for minority students is central to their rates of retention and completion. This aid in turn is a function of the political climate of the times. In December 1990, for example, a furor over scholarships for minority college students was unleashed when a U.S. Department of Education official announced that institutions of higher education receiving federal monies were barred from granting scholarships to specific groups or minorities because such practices constitute discrimination. Although the department's policies were revised within days of the announcement, the issue continued to simmer as conservative groups pressured the Bush administration to eliminate minority scholarship programs. The Clinton administration, however, has brought a renewed spirit of equity that seems to support minority scholarship programs as a path to educational opportunity.

In the same vein, the U.S. Court of Appeals for the Fourth Circuit concluded that past discrimination by a state does not justify a policy of scholarships for minorities. Ironically, the plaintiff in the case was a Hispanic student at the University of Maryland–College Park, who sued the university over a scholarship program targeting African-Americans for financial assistance. The student charged that the university denied his constitutional right to equal protection.

Moreover, intensifying the effects of political and legal attacks on minority scholarships are rising tuition costs and a widespread economic recession. Rising fees and tuition costs will make it more difficult for ethnic minority students to continue their education, especially if minority scholarship programs are curtailed. And as the economic recession continues to force cutbacks in programs at colleges and universities throughout the country, retention programs targeting ethnic minorities will undoubtedly suffer. In this context, new enrollments among Chicanos are likely to decline, attrition rates will probably soar, and the time for completion of a degree will lengthen.

Implications

Trends can often be misleading. Unanticipated social changes occur, and trends are altered and redirected, failing to fulfill one's predictions. Projections that enrollments of Chicanos and other minorities in institutions of higher education will continue to increase, albeit at slower rates, could be reversed if the sociopolitical and economic contexts for ethnic minority groups continue to worsen. On the other hand, a worsening situation demands direct attention, and if political and educational leaders respond effectively to the economic and political problems facing this nation, it could come to be that the status of Chicanos in higher education will actually improve.

Moreover, the continued growth of the Chicano intelligentsia will pass a critical threshold at some point, and the influence of this community will begin to transform institutional practices that deny Chicanos and Chicanas access to and support within institutions of higher education. The Hispanic Association of Colleges and Universities (HACU) has brought the educational plight of Chicanos to the attention of the most prestigious philanthropic organizations in the country (the Ford Foundation and the Sears Roebuck Foundation, for example) and has lobbied the U.S. Congress to set aside funds for colleges and universities whose student populations are comprised of at least 25 percent Hispanic students. While supporters of historically black colleges have opposed this effort, it brings to the fore the fact that the federal government has neglected the educational needs of Chicanos.

Summary

Levels and patterns of Chicanos' participation in postsecondary education in this country indicate their subordinate status in society. They are concentrated in two-year institutions that fail to maintain acceptable levels of completion and transfer rates among students, especially students from low socioeconomic backgrounds. As one moves up the hierarchy of postsecondary educational institutions, one finds fewer and fewer

Chicano and Chicana students. Despite increases in enrollment rates over the past two decades, Chicanos as a group
remain underrepresented in U.S. colleges and universities.

The problem of low enrollments is exacerbated by the gap
between enrollments and completions. Problems of attrition
continue to limit educational achievement among Chicanos
and Chicanas, ensuring that the racial division of labor in the
larger society is maintained. Attrition, however, is a relational
phenomenon, one that exists between students and institutions of higher learning. The sociocultural climates on many
U.S. campuses exclude Chicanos and other ethnic minority
cultures and fail to provide pluralistic climates in which stu
dents develop a sense of integration and belonging.

Overall, enrollment and completion of Chicanos and Chicanas in college demand continued sponsorship by governments, foundations, businesses, and institutions of higher
learning if improvement is to continue. Ultimately, the dropout rate from secondary schools must be reduced, the quality
of education improved, and the educational aspirations of
Chicanos and Chicanas elevated. Community colleges must
improve the quality of education provided to students, and
transfers to four-year institutions must again become central
to their mission. Four-year institutions must recruit and retain
Chicano and Chicana students more aggressively, but to do ·
so effectively, most will have to change the makeup of staff
and faculty, their student academic support programs, and
their sociocultural climates. And graduate schools will have
to do the same.

Ironically, the future of this country will see increasing
dependence on its nonwhite minority populations. If the
United States is to survive as a vibrant sovereign nation, it
must raze all the racial barriers that have kept minorities in
a subordinate position and give them the sociopolitical and
economic space to generate creative solutions to the problems
facing the nation. If it does not effectively use the human
resources available among minorities, the demographic shift
of these populations could serve as the catalyst for the frag-
mentation of the country on the eve of the 21st century.

CHICANO FACULTY IN HIGHER EDUCATION

Estimates of Chicano Faculty

Almost two decades ago, the number of Chicano faculty was estimated at less than 1 percent of the total full-time faculty at institutions of higher education in the United States (Arce 1976). Five years later, Chicano faculty constituted 1.1 percent of the total full-time faculty in the United States (California Postsecondary 1981). According to level of academic appointment, 0.1 percent of Chicano faculty were full professors, 0.3 percent were associate professors, and 0.7 percent were assistant professors. According to table 7, Chicano faculty represented under 1 percent of the U.S. professoriat in fall 1985; further, the representation of Chicano faculty in the professoriat increased as academic rank decreased. A study of trends in the composition of faculty in higher education estimates the number of Chicano faculty in 1989 at 0.8 percent of the total faculty in higher education (Milem and Astin 1993). If one assumes that these estimates are reliable, then the number of Chicano faculty in higher education has not increased appreciably since the estimate in 1976.

In California, a state where Chicanos made up 22 percent of the state's population in 1985, Chicanos constituted 2.4 percent of the faculty in the prestigious University of California system (Garza 1991) (although not too much should be read into that percentage, because it includes persons who identify themselves as either "Hispanic" or "Latino" and, as a result, most likely overrepresents the number of Chicano faculty). An attempt to clarify the limitation on counting Chicano faculty notes that between 1977 and 1987 the number of Chicano faculty at the University of California increased from 171 to 228, while the number of new faculty increased by over 600 during the same period (Haro 1989). While the number of Chicano faculty increased 33 percent between 1977 and 1987, that increase represents an aggregate increase of fewer than six Chicano faculty per year between 1977 and 1987.

Limitations of enumeration

Producing a reliable portrait of Chicano faculty is limited by the process of enumeration. While Hispanics constitute 1.5 percent of all faculty and 1.1 percent of all tenured faculty (Olivas 1988), these statistics are deceptive because they overrepresent the actual number of Chicano faculty. For example, higher education institutions' practices of enumeration hide the small number of Chicano faculty by listing adjunct or

The number of Chicano faculty in higher education may not have increased appreciably since 1976.

TABLE 7
FULL-TIME INSTRUCTIONAL FACULTY IN INSTITUTIONS OF
HIGHER EDUCATION BY GENDER AND CHICANO BACKGROUND: Fall 1985

Academic Rank	U.S. Professoriat (Percent)			Chicano Faculty* (Percent)			Chicano Faculty as Percent of U.S. Professoriat		
	Total	Men	Women	Total	Men	Women	Total	Men	Women
Professor	29.6	35.8	12.8	20.2	23.8	11.6	0.7	0.6	0.9
Associate Professor	25.4	26.7	22.1	23.9	25.3	20.9	0.9	0.9	1.0
Assistant Professor	25.5	22.4	33.9	27.3	26.0	30.5	1.1	1.1	1.0
Instructor	17.3	13.5	27.3	25.1	22.6	30.7	1.4	1.6	1.2
Lecturer	2.2	1.6	3.9	3.5	2.3	6.3	1.6	1.4	1.7
Number	436,000	319,000	117,000	4,300	3,000	1,300			

*Estimated 60 percent of Hispanic population.
Source: National Center for Education Statistics 1991c.

retired faculty as full-time active faculty, identifying professors from Spain and South America as ethnic minority faculty, and counting Anglo women married to Latinos or Chicanos as minority faculty (Olivas 1988). As a result, the population of Chicano/Latino faculty appears larger. In addition, the population of Chicano/Latino faculty appears to grow over time, signaling growing numbers among its ranks. The dilemma for Chicano faculty is that, while the process of enumeration might be increasing the number of entrants into the Chicano/Latino faculty pool, the number of Chicano faculty might not necessarily be increasing. One might even speculate that the number of Chicano faculty in a Chicano/Latino faculty pool decreases with the enumeration process's increased latitude of interpretation for inclusion by group.

The dilemma of identifiability
Limitations in the process of enumerating Chicano faculty, especially grouping Chicano faculty under the label "Hispanic," could amount to a racist practice, because the higher education institution assumes that "they are all the same" (Reyes and Halcon 1988). Similarly, the enumeration of several ethnic groups under the label "Hispanic" ignores "the difference in outlook that each of the subgroups of Hispanic Americans [brings] with [it]" (Nieves-Squires 1992, p. 82)—as well as historical and sociocultural differences. Not only is each subgroup unrecognized, but the grouping of the subgroups also ignores their compatibility with each other.

A review of employment patterns by race and ethnicity in the U.S. professoriat notes that Chicano faculty are concentrated in three areas: humanities, social sciences, and education (National Research Council 1981; see also Martinez 1991). Similarly, a study of Chicano faculty at postsecondary education institutions in the Southwest notes that Chicano faculty in the humanities and social sciences (N = 467) outnumbered Chicano faculty in the sciences and mathematics (N = 86) by a ratio of five to one (Aguirre 1985). Chicano faculty are almost nonexistent in professional programs like dentistry, pharmacy, and engineering (Golladay 1989; U.S. Department of Health and Human Services 1985). Regarding the general distribution of Chicano faculty by academic discipline in academe, "Data gathered by National Chicano Council on Higher Education officials reveal there are only three Chicano professors of higher education, seven physicists, a dozen in chemistry, with slightly greater numbers in sociology, psychology, and bilingual education. By any measure, the numbers are appalling" (Olivas 1988, p. 7).

An example from the social sciences
The small number of Chicano faculty is certainly appalling. One must not assume, however, that the small number of Chicano faculty in certain academic disciplines implies that their number is larger in other academic disciplines. For example, the social sciences are home to a large number of Chicano faculty. An attempt to examine the representation of Chicano faculty in the social sciences focuses on the recruitment and retention of Chicano faculty in political science, identifying 56 Chicano/Latino Ph.D.s in academic political science depart ments as of 1990 (Avalos 1991). The study found that, nationwide, between 1970 and 1980 Ph.D. programs in political science graduated an average of fewer than three Chicanos/ Latinos per year. Of the 56 Chicano/Latino Ph.D.s identified in the study, 13 received the Ph.D. after 1980. Compared to the full-time faculty in political science departments, the 56 Ph.D.s identified in the study represent 0.5 percent of the faculty population. In comparison, Chicano/Latino faculty make up 0.1 to 0.3 percent of the faculty in engineering (National Science Foundation 1989). Thus, Chicano faculty in the social sciences might not be any more representative than Chicano faculty in the sciences.

Institutional Stratification of Chicano Faculty

A few studies have examined Chicano faculty's perceptions of academe, not surprisingly finding that environment isolating, alienating, and exploitative. For example, a study of the impact and use of Chicano faculty within predominately white universities found that Chicano faculty were used to incorporate minor changes in the curriculum but not to play a significant role in making decisions about academic policy (Romero 1977). Chicano faculty could propose course offerings in Chicano studies, but they could not use such course offerings to structure an academic major or program in Chicano studies.

Role perceptions

An examination of the role perceptions held by Chicano administrators in community colleges found that:

1. Chicano administrators experienced a higher degree of role conflict at institutions with 20 percent or fewer Chicano students.
2. Persons who identify themselves as "Chicano" experience a higher degree of role conflict in their role of community college administrator than those identifying themselves as "Mexican American."
3. Chicano administrators believe that their credentials are more carefully scrutinized than those of Anglo administrators.
4. Chicano administrators believe that they are expected to perform at a higher level of competence than Anglo administrators in similar positions.
5. Chicano administrators believe the institution expects them to know everything about Chicanos simply because they are Chicano (Lopez and Schultz 1980).

As a result:

> *A major source of role conflict resulted from the fact that most Chicano administrators are in implementation rather than policy-making roles. . . . Half of these administrators felt personal conflict [as a result of] the fact that their institutions were not responsive enough to Chicano student needs. In fact, the highest ranked source of role conflict related to the fact that these respondents felt tokenism*

toward Chicano student needs was practiced by their insti-
tutions (Lopez and Schultz 1980, p. 53).

Intergroup perceptions

A study of the life experiences that shaped the educational
careers of Chicano students and faculty asked Chicano faculty
to identify problems they had as non-Anglo professionals
(Astin and Burciaga 1981). The Chicano faculty in the study
identified the following problems: (1) a lack of institutional
commitment to educational equality, especially in the recruitment of minority students and faculty; (2) the difficulty in
gaining acceptance and respect from their Anglo colleagues;
and (3) the lack of other minorities at their institution, which
put an extra load on them (that is, the Chicano faculty felt
that they were expected to be institutional watchdogs). "Thus,
Chicano faculty were more likely than were white faculty to
view colleges and universities as racist and were much more
committed to goals of educational equity" (Astin and Burciaga
1981, p. 104).

Opportunity structure

A set of descriptive data regarding the institutional participation of Chicano faculty in academe was used to construct
a set of observations regarding the social context surrounding
Chicano faculty in academe (Aguirre 1987). According to
these observations, the opportunity structure within academe
constrains the participation of Chicano faculty to minority
oriented activities. Further, Chicano faculty are unable to
decrease their participation in university service activities as
they move up the academic ladder.

> *The observations constructed from the results presented sug-*
> *gest the presence of an organizational logic that sorts and*
> *channels Chicano faculty into a limited opportunity struc-*
> *ture in academe. The limitations imposed by this opportu-*
> *nity structure locate Chicano faculty in activities that may*
> *be quite visible, yet are peripheral to the mainstream activity*
> *in the postsecondary organization* (Aguirre 1987, p. 78).

Similarly, a study of Chicano/Latino faculty attitudes toward
the workplace notes that Chicano/Latino faculty perceive
themselves excluded from decision making in their academic
department, believe that the postsecondary institution uses

them as buffers with the minority community, and perceive their campus as not supporting initiatives to improve the campus environment for minority students and faculty (Martinez, Hernandez, and Aguirre *Forthcoming*).

Perceptions of the academic environment
An examination of the perceptions Chicano faculty hold about publication and research in academe found that, while Chicano faculty subscribe to similar scholarly or academic values as white faculty, Chicano faculty believe that university community and research/publication review committees do not accept them as equals or as scholars in their own right (Garza 1989). Further, Chicano faculty believe that their academic research on their own ethnic group is not rated as highly as research conducted by white faculty on Chicanos. Similarly, a study of minority law professors notes that Chicano faculty are often dismissed by white academics from consideration as serious scholars:

> *A Hispanic applied to the LL.M. program at an eminent school to prepare for a teaching career. Although he had graduated from a top law school and first-rate undergraduate university and today is a tenured professor at a top-15 school, the chair of the LL.M. committee told him he would not be admitted because the school reserves its slots for persons of real intellectual caliber* (Delgado 1988, p. 19).

A Portrait of Chicano Faculty
The portrait of Chicano faculty in academe that one can draw from these studies is at best sketchy, and the relatively small number of Chicano faculty in academe limits the amount of detail one can bring to the portrait. But some features in the portrait are rather obvious. For example, there are few Chicano faculty in academe, and those few are concentrated in certain academic disciplines. The paradox is that while one might know where to look for them, one is not certain to find them. Thus, any portrait of Chicano faculty in academe is likely to change, depending on the angle from which one views it. Some prominent features in the portrait remain the same, however, regardless of the angle from which one views the portrait.

Isolation

The institutional relationship between Chicano faculty and administrators in academe places them in a situation of relative isolation, referred to as "barrioization": "Colleges and universities have created a dumping ground for Hispanic scholars, separate from and with little interconnection to the rest of the scholarly life of the university" (Garza 1988, p. 124). In addition, the institutional isolation of Chicano faculty is enhanced by an opportunity structure that shifts their institutional participation to peripheral activities (Aguirre 1987).

Exclusion

Two factors contribute to the relative isolation of Chicano faculty in academe: overloading Chicano faculty with minority-oriented institutional demands, such as service on university minority affairs committees, and the lack of an established institutional network for Chicano faculty that could sponsor them within a variety of institutional sectors apart from minority-oriented activities (Escobedo 1980). Chicano faculty feel constrained by institutional demands that prevent them from participating in institutional sectors that are closer to mainstream decision making (Garza 1989; Lopez and Schultz 1980).

In a sense, then, the relative isolation of Chicano faculty in academe has made them victims of "academic colonialism," because:

> *Whether one refers to Chicano institutions or Chicano programs or Chicano personnel or students, the norm is for the organizational loci of them to be in the periphery, in terms of participation in governance, academic credibility, recognition and status, resource allocation, permanence, and facilities* (Arce 1978, p. 86).

As peripheral participants in academe, Chicano faculty are unable to develop networks that could alter the perceptions white faculty hold of them.

As peripheral participants in academe, Chicano faculty are unable to develop networks that could alter the perceptions white faculty hold of them. The inability of Chicano faculty to alter those perceptions contributes to their neglect within academe. That is, white faculty will maintain the peripheral status of Chicano faculty by ignoring them. As a result, the actions of white faculty produce an institutional form of discrimination that impedes the progress of Chicano faculty in academe (Reyes and Halcon 1991). In turn, the institutional discrimination serves to preserve academe as a domain for white males (Bell 1986; Bunzel 1990; Valverde 1975). Perhaps gains made by white women in academe relative to affirmative action have been at the expense of minority men (Cortese 1992b), and as such, academe could be the domain of both white males and white females.

A comparative note

For the purpose of comparison, we must note how Chicano faculty compare with other minority and women faculty in academe. Chicano faculty share similar experiences with other minority and women faculty in their interactions with the postsecondary institution (Aguirre, Martinez, and Hernandez 1993). In particular, Chicano faculty share similar levels of dissatisfaction with other minority and women faculty regarding the workplace in academe in that they feel excluded from mainstream decision making and find themselves overloaded with activities that target their status, such as race, ethnicity, and/or gender (Hu-Dehart 1983; Lopez 1991; Nieves-Squires 1991). As a result, it appears that Chicano faculty, like other minority and women faculty, occupy an organizational niche that enhances their powerless position in academe. This position of powerlessness becomes more acute if one assumes that exclusion from mainstream academic activities limits the social power and influence one can exert in academe.

Dilemmas in Academe for Chicano Faculty

Using the research literature on Chicano faculty, we can make some observations about the dilemmas Chicano faculty face in academe. In general, the contextual feature of the post-secondary education institution's environment that best characterizes the status of Chicano faculty is *exclusion*. The number of Chicano faculty in academe is too small for them to demand institutional changes, but it is large enough to facilitate their use by the institution. The contextual character of Chicano faculty in academe is best summed up as follows:

> *As a Chicano law professor, I fully appreciate the extent to which I and Latino colleagues have greater responsibilities; our service contributions and informal duties at times seem overwhelming. However, unless higher education takes more seriously its responsibilities to seek out others like us, and to behave differently toward Latinos, the extraordinary cycle*

of exclusion from faculty ranks will continue. Higher edu-
cation is poorer for its loss (Olivas 1988, p. 9).

Thus, the nature of the exclusion of Chicano faculty is not
limited to their invisibility within faculty ranks; it also affects
their ability to identify with the environment of the postsecondary institution. The exclusionary practices Chicano faculty
face in academe are the bases for creating dilemmas in their
participation as faculty members.

Institutional acceptance and accommodation
The entry of Chicano faculty into academe will continue to
be an uphill journey, because white faculty are unwilling to
accept Chicano faculty—and other minority faculty—into their
ranks (Bell 1986; Willie 1988). One result of this unwilling-
ness is minority faculty's continued treatment as peripheral
participants in academe (Delgado 1988; Exum 1983; Smith
and Witt 1990; Witt 1990). While the peripheral treatment of
minority faculty might suggest that white faculty tolerate their
presence—after all, they are not completely excluded from
academe—it does show that white faculty resist the entry of
minority faculty into academe. What does it mean for Chicano
faculty?

One must keep in mind that Chicano faculty have embarked on "extraordinary careers" because they have managed
to transcend the social expectations ascribed to their minority
status in U.S. society. These extraordinary careers have
enabled Chicano faculty to acquire the credentials to seek
access to academe—a paradise consisting of positions with
high social value. Some of the literature reviewed for this
monograph suggests that they are treated as strangers in academe. To make their presence in academe legitimate, the
postsecondary institution makes "sense" of their presence
by supporting an opportunity structure that channels their
participation to institutional sectors and activities focused on
minority issues.

From an institutional perspective, the postsecondary institution sends two signals to white faculty from Chicanos' participation in minority-oriented activities: (1) the institutional
use of Chicano faculty to serve others like them, namely Chicano students; and (2) the use of Chicano faculty to address
the institution's need to offer an ethnically diverse curriculum.
As a result, individual white faculty members perceive Chi-

cano faculty as strangers and, more important, not as competitors in the distribution of resources within the institution's mainstream activities. The dilemma for Chicano faculty then is that if persons who embark on extraordinary careers are treated this way in academe, how will they convince other Chicanos and Chicanas to embark on their own extraordinary careers in academe?

Faculty development

As peripheral participants in academe, Chicano faculty are excluded from the postsecondary institution's mainstream activities. The relative position of Chicano faculty on the lower rungs of the academic ladder constrains their ability to gain access to sectors of influence within academe. For example, while minority faculty are underrepresented at all levels of the tenure track, between 1972 and 1989 the largest proportion of Chicano faculty was found at the rank of assistant professor (Milem and Astin 1993). In addition, the institution's expectation for Chicano faculty to participate in minority-oriented activities tends to remove them from serving in other institutional sectors or activities—as department chair or on personnel review committees, merit/promotion committees, or tenure review committees, for example (Aguirre 1985). Consequently, limiting Chicano faculty to minority-oriented sectors or activities also limits their ability to develop an institutional network that sponsors their presence within academe. In particular, this institutional network would be instrumental in establishing continuity within the academic ranks for Chicano faculty, not unlike the old boy network among white male faculty.

Second, the inability of Chicano faculty to use their academic presence to remove ambiguity from the institutional interpretation of their behavior has placed them in a difficult position in academe: to be or not to be Chicano. Postsecondary institutions *expect* Chicano faculty to actualize their person by maintaining links with the Chicano community (in service activities) and its representatives (the students), yet they expect Chicano faculty to function as institutional members subscribing to the ideals of teaching and research (Aguirre 1981). As a result, Chicano faculty are ascribed a dual identity within academe that requires tremendous amounts of time and energy to actualize. In contrast, white faculty are not

expected to have a dual identity, because they do not need
to justify their presence in academe.

> *Hispanic and other minority faculty members are forced
> to assume more responsibility than their nonminority faculty
> counterparts by rendering service to the minority commu-
> nity and assistance to minority students and by serving on
> department, college, and university committees to represent
> minority interests. . . . The traditional triangular criteria
> of teaching, research, and service . . . and added respon-
> sibilities of Hispanic faculty members in the area of service
> unfairly [handicap] their chances for promotion and ten-
> ure* (Valverde 1981, p. 59).

Academia is the context within which white faculty enhance
their institutional visibility. But it is the context that segments
Chicano faculty to the point of making them invisible.

One attribute of maintaining a dual identity is that it
requires Chicano faculty to serve as role models for both the
minority community and the academic community. While
the concept of role models has attracted tremendous interest
in academe, minority faculty should not serve as role models
in academe for five reasons:

> *Reason Number One. Being a role model is a tough job, with
> long hours and much heavy lifting. You are expected to
> uplift your entire people. Talk about hard, sweaty work!*
>
> *Reason Number Two. The job treats you as a means to
> an end. Even your own constituency may begin to see you
> this way. "Of course Tanya will agree to serve as our faculty
> advisor, give this speech, serve on that panel, or agree to do
> us X, Y, or Z favor, probably unpaid and on short notice.
> What is her purpose if not to serve us?"*
>
> *Reason Number Three. The role model's job description
> is monumentally unclear. If highway workers or tax asses-
> sors had such unclear job descriptions, they would strike.
> If you are a role model, are you expected to do the same
> things your white counterpart does, in addition to coun-
> seling and helping out the community of color whenever
> something comes up?*
>
> *Reason Number Four. To be a good role model, you must
> be an assimilationist, never a cultural or economic*

nationalist, separatist, radical reformer, or anything
remotely resembling any of [them].

Reason Number Five (the most important one). The job
of role model requires that you lie—that you tell not little,
but big, whopping lies—and that is bad for your soul. Sup-
pose I am sent out to an inner city school to talk to the kids
and serve as a role model of the month. I am expected to
tell the kids that if they study hard and stay out of trouble,
they can become a law professor like me. That, however,
is a very big lie. . . . Fortunately, most kids are smart enough
to figure out that the system does not work this way. If I were
honest, I would advise them to become major league baseball
players, or to practice their hook shots. As Michael Olivas points
out, the odds, pay, and working conditions are much better
in these other lines of work (Delgado 1991, pp. 1227–29).

The dual identity is a dilemma for Chicano faculty: Whose
interests does one represent in academe? and when?

Academic politics
From the institution's point of view, the best vehicle for
enhancing a faculty member's role in academic politics is tenure and promotion. Institutional expectations built in to the
dual identity of Chicano faculty hamper them in securing tenure and promotion, however.

The trouble is not due to lack of productivity or competency,
but rather to criteria application. The conventional criteria
applied during tenure review are interpreted by nonmi-
nority faculty members in such a way as to not accept His-
panic faculty activities (mainly service to university and
the field) as fulfilling the criteria (Valverde 1981, p. 52).

Without a significant number of Chicano faculty in tenured
and senior faculty positions, Chicano faculty will not be able
to enter an institutional network that enhances their role as
political brokers in academe. For example, because participation in some of the most powerful faculty senate committees is often limited to tenured senior faculty, the inability
of Chicanos to move into those ranks prevents them from participating in institutional activities that allocate resources, such
as research grants. As participants in those activities, Chicano
faculty could use the allocation of resources to sponsor un-

tenured Chicano faculty in academe. That is, tenured Chicano faculty could facilitate the untenured Chicano faculty member's access to research grants. In turn, research support not only permits an untenured faculty member to pursue a research program, but also enhances his or her chances for tenure and promotion.

Can Chicano faculty become viable political agents in academe? In general, for Chicano faculty to become viable political agents in academe, the opportunity structure that allocates privilege and power must be restructured. The chances that this change will occur are almost zero (Bunzel 1990; Trow 1992), but other correlates of Chicano faculty's presence in academe suggest their viability as political agents. First, the exclusion of Chicano faculty from certain academic sectors and activities has resulted in a sense of "institutional marginality" among Chicano faculty, which in turn has facilitated postsecondary institutions' system of institutional discrimination regarding their participation in an institutional network necessary to build powerful alliances.

Second, the cognitive impact of institutional marginality is that Chicano faculty might perceive of themselves as "tokens" in academe (Phillips and Blumberg 1983). Even though Chicano faculty hold similar scholarly values as white faculty, Chicano faculty feel that white faculty do not perceive Chicano faculty as legitimate participants in academe (Garza 1991). Rather, white faculty perceive Chicano faculty as participants in academe as a result of institutional needs to meet external demands (such as affirmative action). If Chicano faculty and white faculty see Chicano faculty as tokens, then Chicano faculty will hesitate to participate in institutional activities or sectors that bestow political legitimacy. The issue is compounded for Chicano faculty, because white faculty serve as the primary gatekeepers for those institutional sectors or activities.

If Chicano faculty are to become viable political agents in academe, certain structural and institutional issues must be addressed. First, the hierarchical arrangement of privilege and power in academe must be restructured to provide Chicano faculty with access. Second, Chicano faculty must increase their numbers within the tenured ranks of the faculty. Third, white faculty must alter their perception that Chicano faculty are tokens and are present in academe only as a result of external demands on academe. While attaining these conditions does not guarantee how academe will respond to or treat Chicano faculty, it does serve as a vehicle for changing the contextual participation of Chicano faculty in academe.

Summary

The number of Chicano faculty is still rather small, and the population of Chicano faculty has not grown appreciably in almost two decades. As a result, Chicano faculty are still relatively new entrants to academe. Further, institutions tend to exclude Chicano faculty from participation in academe. By using an opportunity structure that focuses Chicano faculty's participation in minority-oriented activities, postsecondary institutions exclude Chicano faculty from mainstream activities. In turn, those exclusionary practices make Chicano faculty peripheral participants. In a sense, Chicano faculty are victims of "academic colonialism"; that is, Chicano faculty exist only as fabricated actors that meet the institutional needs and demands of academe.

Finally, the nature of their participation in academe creates a number of dilemmas for Chicano faculty. Their treatment as peripheral participants makes it difficult for them to sponsor Chicano students. The relatively powerless position of Chicano faculty prevents them from establishing an institutional network that could result in powerful academic alliances. The ascription of a dual identity for Chicano faculty enhances their invisibility by forcing them to participate in institutional activities or sectors white faculty do not regard as legitimate vehicles for tenure and promotion.

THE EDUCATION OF CHICANOS IN THE 21st CENTURY

As we approach the 21st century, U.S. society finds itself renewing interest in educational opportunity for its minority populations. That renewed interest reflects a single reality: the link between the future of the U.S. economy and the socioeconomic future of minority populations. Not since the civil rights movement of the 1960s has U.S. society stirred visibly in the area of educational opportunity for its minority populations. The tide of neoconservatism of the late 1970s that manifested itself as an attack on minority-related educational programs throughout U.S. society generated a sociopolitical climate that no longer tolerated efforts to break down racial and ethnic barriers in society. The 1980s, as a result, became the decade in which social action programs, such as affirmative action, came under attack for actually promoting equal opportunity for racial and ethnic minorities. What then of the 1990s? Will minority populations in the United States experience greater educational opportunity?

Not since the civil rights movement of the 1960s has U.S. society stirred visibly in the area of educational opportunity for its minority populations.

The Educational Arena

The educational arena continues to be the most visible context for promoting equal opportunity for racial and ethnic populations in the United States. The educational system in U.S. society is the vehicle minority populations can use to increase their socioeconomic mobility. The association between schooling and the opportunity structure in society has occurred by design, not by accident: "Early education reformers believed that by opening schools up to those who had traditionally been denied access (e.g., minorities and the poor) and by instilling in them the values of the dominant society, they could lessen social inequalities and encourage social mobility" (Walsh 1987, p. 127).

Equality of educational opportunity, then, is an important concern for minority populations, because it has the potential to alter their social inequality in U.S. society. Equality of educational opportunity also serves as a vehicle by which U.S. society can ensure a relative degree of stability in its socioeconomic infrastructure by providing its minority populations with socioeconomic mobility through educational attainment. Thus, it is in the best interest of U.S. society to promote and enhance educational opportunity for its minority populations.

The Chicano Population

The Chicano population is growing in number. Whether one views such growth as the product of immigration from Mexico, a high birthrate in the Chicano population, or shrinking numbers in the white population, one can no longer ignore the full impact of the Chicano population in the United States (Chapa and Valencia 1993). U.S. society as a whole, however, might not experience the full impact of the emergence of the Chicano population. "The reality is . . . that the plight of Chicanos directly affects a significant portion of the population of the Southwest and less directly affects everyone else in the country" (Gandara 1986, p. 259). Educational institutions, however, will feel the full impact of the emerging Chicano population (Hyland 1992).

> *There is a critical challenge facing U.S. public school educators. There is a steadily increasing Hispanic student population, one that demographers predict will eclipse the current black population of school children within the next generation. This is coupled with data suggesting that Hispanic students are the most "undereducated" of all major population groups in terms of educational attainment* (Hyland 1992, pp. 138–39).

As noted earlier, the undereducation of the Chicano population seriously undermines its socioeconomic mobility in U.S. society. The situation becomes alarming when one considers that the Chicano population is entering the 21st century undereducated and uneducated.

The Context for Educational Change

Perhaps the best way to approach a discussion of the context for educational change for Chicanos is by reviewing some examples of what other researchers and educators have identified as critical initiatives. For purposes of this discussion, the initiatives are divided into two general categories: *processual,* initiatives that focus on changing the manner in which Chicano students are processed by educational institutions, and *structural,* initiatives that focus on altering the relationship of Chicano students to the school structure. These two categories are by no means exclusive of each other. They are used only as a tool with which to discuss the micro (processual) and macro (structural) features of the context for Chicano education.

Processual initiatives for kindergarten through grade 12

The following two educational features need to be changed for schools to meet the needs of Chicano students:

1. *Tracking*. Change the practice of grouping or tracking students by examining alternatives to the use of standardized tests that are culturally and linguistically biased against Chicano students.
2. *Language instruction*. Implement English-language instruction for Chicanos who speak limited English that will prevent them from falling behind their classmates and, as a result, dropping out of school in large numbers (Gandara 1986; Hyland 1992).

Changing these two areas has the potential to reduce the educational abuse of Chicano students and their families:

> *The consequences of educational abuse are devastating for Chicano children. . . . Educational abuse condemns its victims to a life of poverty and denies them the social mobility that is primarily achieved through public education. It also manifests itself in gross insensitivity to the needs of these youths, especially in the areas of culture and language and in the absence of specific programs to address such needs* (Arevalo and Brown 1983, p. 157).

Structural initiatives for kindergarten through grade 12

Despite the growing number of Chicano students in kindergarten through grade 12, Chicano teachers of those grades are in increasingly short supply (Monsivais 1990). Public schools would be more effective in teaching Chicano students if they had adequate numbers of trained and qualified Chicano teachers, thereby increasing the chances of incorporating Chicano students into the school structure. By serving as role models, for example, Chicano teachers can encourage Chicano students to pursue educational goals, and Chicano students' incorporation into the school structure enhances their chances of progressing through the educational system.

Further, educational intervention programs must be implemented to target Chicano students interested in pursuing a college degree (De Necochea 1988). To be successful, such programs must:

1. Focus on the early identification of students for a college preparatory curriculum;
2. Improve students' preparation in math and science;
3. Encourage schools to create an environment that makes activities for the college bound visible;
4. Strengthen the link between the school and college recruiters;
5. Provide students with college prep workshops;
6. Encourage parents to participate in these workshops with their children; and
7. Centralize the location of college information in the school (De Necochea 1988).

The goal of intervention programs for college-bound Chicano students is to create a pool of Chicano students that increases over time as the population itself grows over time. In the end, the number of Chicano college students would increase steadily over time, rather than by spurts.

In sum, the alteration of features like tracking and language instruction will transform the personal relationship of Chicanos to the school, and the transformation will in turn alter Chicano students' perception of the school from oppressive to opportunistic. The alteration of structural features, such as the availability of Chicano teachers and intervention programs for college-bound Chicano students, will change the structural relationship of Chicano students in school, and Chicano students will identify with the school's structure by perceiving educational growth as a process of attainment rather than one of exclusion. The alteration of processual and structural features together will transform educational institutions into vehicles for social change, rather than casualties of social change, for the Chicano population in the 21st century.

Educational Change at the Postsecondary Level

Educational initiatives at the postsecondary level focusing on minority students have not succeeded because postsecondary institutions believe that social inequality does not exist within their confines:

> Nearly 15 years of civil rights legislation have not substantially improved the condition of minority education, while, ironically, the prevailing illusion of substantially increased access has forestalled necessary changes in existing systems.

Thus, minorities and other underrepresented groups find themselves underserved by programs designed to redress inequities and ill served by a popular notion that inequities no longer exist (Olivas 1984, p. 89).

Similarly, a review of reform initiatives for higher education and their effect on minority youth notes:

It is not surprising, then, that major reforms were proposed and implemented with little thought given to their potentially negative effects on minorities. If the content and direction of the current reform reports are any indication of what awaits minorities in the future, the prospects for improving their educational condition appear dim (Halcon and Reyes 1991, p. 118).

Thus, reform initiatives in postsecondary education for minority students could create more problems than solutions. Despite academia's potential to create a better understanding of the social inequality facing racial and ethnic minorities in U.S. society, the politics of neoconservatism that pervade academia often results in the rejection of racial and ethnic minorities as faculty or students (Trueba 1993).

The problematic nature of reform initiatives for minority students in postsecondary education can also signal their vulnerability. In some instances, for example, reform initiatives supporting minority students in postsecondary education have become weapons with which white society argues that it has become the new victim. In other instances, reform initiatives have created a concern in white society that postsecondary institutions are compromising their educational quality (Astin 1990). As a result, postsecondary institutions find themselves in a quandary regarding the recruitment and support of minority students.

Processual initiatives
In general, postsecondary institutions are raising their admission standards so that fewer students are being admitted as exceptions to formal academic requirements. This practice poses a problem for Chicanos, for the unequal educational opportunities encountered by Chicanos create a context in which college-bound Chicano students tend to have lower high school grade point averages and lower scores on stan-

dardized tests. While this context can be perceived as placing Chicanos at a disadvantage, studies that have examined the retention rate of Chicano college students suggest that personal, nonacademic qualities like self-esteem, leadership ability, and community involvement often play a more important role in college persistence for Chicano students. Consequently, a shift in college admissions from the predominant use of standardized test scores and high school GPA to an examination of a student's personal qualities could result in more opportunity for Chicano students.

Second, the costs of a postsecondary education have increased substantially over the past few years. Despite the positive effects of financial aid for students upon students' persistence in college (Cabrera, Stampen, and Hansen 1990; Nora 1990; Stampen and Cabrera 1988), financial aid continues to be the target of budget cutbacks. In addition, the emphasis has shifted from grant aid to loans and work-study programs, eligibility criteria for student aid have been raised, and the application process now requires considerably more paperwork. The shift from grants to loans and work-study programs, in particular, presents problems for Chicano students, because research indicates that grants rather than loans are associated with staying in college. The institutional practice of employing federal aid, especially grants, for Chicano students places them at risk when federal cutbacks in financial aid programs are implemented (Olivas 1985, 1986a). In turn, the presence and continuity of Chicano college students are at risk as a result of inequities created by bureaucratic and legislative action. Thus, financial aid packages for Chicano students must be developed that foster educational continuity rather than placing it at risk.

Structural initiatives

Research suggests that the retention of Chicano students in postsecondary institutions is associated with the availability of student support services that facilitate their adaptation to a relatively new and alien environment (Chavez 1986)— among them tutorial and remedial learning programs, specialized academic counseling and orientation sessions, and social support programs. Institutional resources for these programs, however, have been decreasing over time, and it does not appear likely that the direction will change in the near future. Postsecondary institutions need to commit resources that will create a supportive environment for student services. It is useless to have student support services for Chicano students if those services are the first victims during budget cutbacks. If student support services are to increase the presence of Chicano students in postsecondary institutions, then institutions must commit resources that will insulate them from becoming the first casualties of budget cutbacks.

Second, although one of the major goals of two-year colleges is to prepare students to undertake work at a four-year institution, few two-year college students, especially minority students, go on to study at four-year institutions. Part of the dilemma of transferring from a two-year college to a four-year institution involves the lack of coordinated requirements, the lack of uniformity in course offerings, and different policies for assessment (Olivas 1979). The potential loss of credits in transferring from a two-year college to a four-year institution is a factor in whether a minority student will transfer (Pincus and DeCamp 1989). In general, the transfer rate for Chicano students at two year colleges to four-year institutions is about 6 percent, and their attrition rate is higher at two-year institutions than at four-year institutions (de los Santos, Montemayor, and Solis 1983; Rendon and Nora 1989).

The transfer of Chicano students from two-year colleges to four year institutions is important because most Chicano college students are enrolled at two-year colleges. Two-year and four-year institutions must develop a closer collaboration to increase not only the transfer rate between them, but also the retention rate of Chicano students at two-year institutions. If two-year institutions are to feed Chicano students effectively to four-year institutions, they must develop strategies that will retain and prepare Chicanos for the transfer. Closer collaboration between two-year and four-year institutions would go far in making the transfer process less ambiguous for Chicano students.

The third structural initiative—perhaps the concept used most frequently today in attempting to retain Chicano college students—is that of role model. Providing more Chicano faculty would help postsecondary institutions increase their retention rates for Chicano students. It is clear that the number of minority faculty at an institution is positively related to the retention of minority students. Whether it is because students struggle to be like their mentors or because their mentors treat them with empathy and respect is not clear, but the mentoring role of minority faculty is critical. Unfortunately, Chicano faculty, like other minority faculty, are aboard an academic merry-go-round, having to teach at several institutions before they can obtain a tenure-track position, then moving to another institution after being denied tenure. Postsecondary institutions need to recruit and retain Chicano faculty to provide Chicano college students with visible products of educational growth and to guide Chicano students into graduate and professional study.

In sum, the processual and structural initiatives at the postsecondary level target *access* as a significant obstacle to the educational pursuits of Chicano students. Student support services are the best vehicle for creating a supportive institutional environment for Chicano students, but Chicano faculty must be recruited to provide Chicano students with role models that can motivate them to pursue graduate and professional study. These initiatives have the potential to alter Chicanos' access to higher education, changing the context that currently shapes their participation in higher education.

Chicanos and Educational Policy
One of the realities of minority status in U.S. society is the exclusion a person faces in everyday life. The exclusion covers a wide range of behaviors and situations, from being ignored by a salesperson to being ignored by educational policy makers. One reason that minority persons are excluded from policy making is that they are often focused on fighting problems created for them by others; thus, minorities are often victims of their own victimization. Minorities often feel powerless in decision making:

> *Disadvantaged interest groups seem to find themselves constantly reacting to new crises not of their own creation because they are not in a position of authority to formulate policies reflective of their own interests or to enforce present policies in ways . . . they deem appropriate. Thus, they are constrained and, for the most part, powerless to influence the policy-making process, except through reactive counter-efforts and campaigns* (Arciniega 1982, p. 125).

Second, minority persons have been excluded because educational policy makers believe that educational quality and minority status are not compatible; that is, minority persons lower educational quality rather than educational quality reduces minority status.

> *Much of the literature and rhetoric of the reform movement leaves the impression that increasing minority populations in the public schools and open access to higher education over the last two decades are the central cause[s] of the decline in the quality of higher education. . . . The assumption made by most reformers is that excellence and equity are incompatible, or mutually exclusive* (Halcon and Reyes 1991, pp. 131–32).

Finally, the exclusion of minority persons is reinforced by a widely held belief that "things have improved" for them. "Could equity have possibly been achieved for minorities in education and therefore become insignificant in the minds of policy leaders?" (Ginsberg and Bennett 1989, p. 257). As noted earlier, despite gains in educational outcomes for Chicanos, the Chicano population lags behind other racial and ethnic populations in educational outcomes. Are the gains in educational outcomes a signal that the Chicano population has attained educational equity, despite the fact that the majority of the Chicano population has not completed at least four years of high school? Should one be optimistic about the Chicano population's educational outcomes? No. "Optimism is unwarranted because of a verifiable decline in minority access, because of a changed mood in larger communities concerning access, and because of continued intransigence on the part of institutions" (Olivas 1984, p. 85).

Given the beliefs surrounding the exclusion of minorities from policy making and the misplaced optimism for minority education, what role can Chicanos play in educational policy making? Before Chicanos can participate in educational policy making, their socioeconomic position within U.S. society must be transformed. They must acquire a socioeconomic position that will provide them with the legitimacy for entering policy-making arenas—from a position of relative disadvantage to one of relative advantage in policy making. If such a transformation were to occur for the Chicano population, then a policy and research agenda could be developed that focuses on:

> *(1) the development of important baseline human research data regarding the status of Hispanics in various professions*

*and occupations in both the public and private sectors, (2)
the consideration of policy research and related study
efforts across existing centers, institutes, and agencies, (3)
the identification in timely fashion of major issues on public
policy impacting on Chicanos and the development of alternative policies, and (4) the development of coordinated
dissemination of information and training activities to
inform and educate our people in these issues as they
unfold* (Arciniega 1982, p. 135).

In reality, it is unclear what role Chicanos can and will play
in educational policy making. The isolation and neglect Chicanos have experienced, and continue to experience, within
the U.S. educational system constrain the population's ability
to use the educational process as a vehicle for personal and
social change. Without educational credentials, for example,
the population runs the risk of not being able to enter the
sectors in U.S. society that can transform its socioeconomic
position. The 21st century will be a testing ground for Chicanos: They will either marshal themselves for entry into
policy-making arenas, or they will continue to be ignored in
policy making.

Summary

U.S. society has renewed its interest in educational opportunity for its minorities. As these populations have continued
to grow in number and the number of white retirement-age
persons has increased, U.S. society has increased its social
and economic dependence on minority populations. The educational arena has become the most visible context for providing minorities with equal opportunity. Equal educational
opportunity for Chicanos has focused on several initiatives
that attempt to enhance their participation in education and
access to postsecondary institutions. But for educational
access to change for Chicanos, the context surrounding Chicano education must change. The Chicano population must
change its socioeconomic position in U.S. society from one
of relative disadvantage to one of relative advantage—with
the result that Chicanos would increase their chances of
influencing policy.

REFERENCES

The Educational Resources Information Center (ERIC) Clearinghouse on Higher Education abstracts and indexes the current literature on higher education for inclusion in ERIC's data base and announcement in ERIC's monthly bibliographic journal, *Resources in Education* (RIE). Most of these publications are available through the ERIC Document Reproduction Service (EDRS). For publications cited in this bibliography that are available from EDRS, ordering number and price code are included. Readers who wish to order a publication should write to the ERIC Document Reproduction Service, 7420 Fullerton Rd., Suite 110, Springfield, VA 22153-2852. (Phone orders with VISA or MasterCard are taken at 800-443-ERIC or 703-440-1400.) When ordering, please specify the document (ED) number. Documents are available as noted in microfiche (MF) and paper copy (PC). If you have the price code ready when you call EDRS, an exact price can be quoted. The last page of the latest issue of *Resources in Education* also has the current cost, listed by code.

Acevedo, B. 1979. "Socialization: Chicano Administrators in Higher Education." *Emergent Leadership* 3: 28–41.

Acuña, R. 1992. "Chicano Studies: A Public Trust." In *Chicano Studies: Critical Connection between Research and Community*, edited by T. Cordova. San Antonio: National Association of Chicano Studies.

Aguirre, A., Jr. 1979. "Intelligence Testing and Chicanos: A Quality of Life Issue." *Social Problems* 27: 186–95.

———. 1980. *Intelligence Testing, Education, and Chicanos.* ERIC/TM Report 76. Princeton, N.J.: ERIC Clearinghouse on Tests, Measurement, and Evaluation. ED 198 153. 62 pp. MF–01; PC not available EDRS.

———. 1981. "Chicano Faculty in Postsecondary Educational Institutions." *California Journal of Teacher Education* 8: 11–19.

———. 1985. "Chicano Faculty at Postsecondary Educational Institutions in the Southwest." *Journal of Educational Equity and Leadership* 5: 133–44.

———. 1987. "An Interpretative Analysis of Chicano Faculty in Academe." *Social Science Journal* 24: 71–81.

Aguirre, A., Jr., and R. Martinez. 1984. "Hispanics and the U.S. Occupational Structure: A Focus on Vocational Education." *International Journal of Sociology and Social Policy* 4: 50–59.

Aguirre, A., Jr., R. Martinez, and A. Hernandez. 1993. "Majority and Minority Faculty Perspectives in Academe." *Research in Higher Education* 34: 371–85.

Alvarez, R. 1979. "Institutional Discrimination in Organizations and Their Environments." In *Discrimination in Organizations,* edited by R. Alvarez, K. Lutterman, and Associates. San Francisco: Jossey-Bass.

Amaury, N. 1990. "Campus-based Aid Programs as Determinants of

Retention among Hispanic Community College Students." *Journal of Higher Education* 61: 312–31.

Amaury, N., and F. Horvath. 1989. "Financial Assistance: Minority Enrollments and Persistence." *Education and Urban Society* 21: 299–311.

Arbona, C., and D. Novy. 1990. "Noncognitive Dimensions as Predictors of College Success among Black, Mexican American, and White Students." *Journal of College Student Development* 31: 415–22.

Arce, C. 1976. "Chicanos in Higher Education." *Integrated Education* 14: 14–18.

———. 1978. "Chicano Participation in Academe: A Case of Academic Colonialism." *Grito del Sol: A Chicano Quarterly* 3: 75–104.

———. 1981. "A Reconsideration of Chicano Culture and Identity." *Daedalus* 110: 177–91.

Arciniega, T. 1982. "A Research Agenda for Hispanic Policy." In *Hispanics in Higher Education: Leadership and Vision for the next 25 Years,* edited by L. Valverde and S. Garcia. Austin: Univ. of Texas at Austin, Office for Advanced Research in Hispanic Education.

Arevalo, R., and J. Brown. 1983. "Educational Abuse of Chicano Youths." *Social Work Education* 5: 156–64.

Arizona Association of Chicanos for Higher Education. 1984. *An Action Plan for Chicano Higher Education in Arizona.* Tucson: Univ. of Arizona, Mexican American Studies and Research Center.

Astin, A. 1982. *Minorities in American Higher Education.* San Francisco: Jossey-Bass.

———. 1990. "Educational Assessment and Educational Equity." *American Journal of Education* 98: 458–78.

Astin, H., and C. Burciaga. 1981. *Chicanos in Higher Education: Progress and Attainment.* ED 226 690. 179 pp. MF–01; PC–08.

Avalos, M. 1991. "The Status of Latinos in the Profession: Problems in Recruitment and Retention." *PS: Political Science and Politics* 24: 241–46.

Barkley, S. 1993. "A Synthesis of Recent Literature on Articulation and Transfer." *Community College Review* 20: 38–50.

Barry, P. 1991. "Interview. A New Voice for Hispanics in Higher Education: A Conversation with Antonio Rigual." *College Board Review* 160: 2–7.

Bean, F., and M. Tienda. 1987. *The Hispanic Population of the United States.* New York: Russell Sage Foundation.

Bell, D. 1986. "Strangers in Academic Paradise: Law Teachers of Color in Still White Schools." *University of San Francisco Law Review* 20: 385–95.

Bender, L. 1991. "Minority Transfer: A National and State Legislative Perspective." *New Directions for Community Colleges* 19: 69–75.

Bonilla, F., and R. Campos. 1981. "A Wealth of Poor: Puerto Ricans in the New Economic Order." *Daedalus* 110: 133–76.

Brischetto, R., and T. Arciniega. 1973. "Examining the Examiners:
A Look at Educators' Perspectives on the Chicano Student." In *Chicanos and Native Americans: The Territorial Minorities,* edited
by R. de la Garza, Z. Kruszewski, and T. Arciniega. Englewood
Cliffs, N.J.: Prentice-Hall.

Brown, G., N. Rosen, S. Hill, and M. Olivas. 1980. *The Condition of
Education for Hispanic Americans.* Washington, D.C.: U.S. Government Printing Office.

Brown, S. 1987. *Minorities in the Graduate Education Pipeline.*
Princeton, N.J.: Educational Testing Service, Minority Graduate Education Project.

Bunzel, J. 1990. "Minority Faculty Hiring: Problems and Prospects."
American Scholar 59: 39–52.

Caballero, C., ed. 1985. *Chicano Organizations Directory.* New York:
Neal-Schuman Publishers.

Cabrera, A., J. Stampen, and W. Hansen. 1990. "Exploring the Effects
of Ability to Pay on Persistence in College." *Review of Higher Education* 13: 308–36.

Cabrera, Y. 1970. *Minorities in Higher Education: Chicanos and Others.* Niwot, Colo.: Sierra Publications.

Cage, M. 26 May 1993. "Graduation Rates of American Indians and
Blacks Improve, Lag behind Others." *Chronicle of Higher Education.* A29–A30.

California Advisory Committee to the U.S. Commission on Civil
Rights. 1977. *Evaluation of Educable Mentally Retarded Programs
in California.* Washington, D.C.: U.S. Government Printing Office.

California Legislature. 1985. *The Undereducation of Minorities and
the Impact on the California Economy.* Sacramento: California
Joint Publications Office.

California Postsecondary Education Commission. 1981. *Women and
Minorities in California Public Postsecondary Education.* Sacramento: Author. ED 230 086. 228 pp. MF–01; PC–10.

California State University. 1984. *Hispanics and Higher Education:
A CSU Imperative.* Long Beach: California State Univ., Commission
on Hispanic Underrepresentation.

California State University and Colleges. 1978. *A Framework for Student Affirmative Action in the California State University and Colleges.* Long Beach: Office of the Chancellor.

Carter, D., and R. Wilson. 1989. *Minorities in Higher Education.*
Eighth Annual Status Report. Washington, D.C.: American Council
on Education, Office of Minorities in Higher Education. ED 320
510. 56 pp. MF–01; PC–03.

———. 1991. *Minorities in Higher Education.* Ninth Annual Status
Report. Washington, D.C.: American Council on Education, Office
of Minorities in Higher Education. ED 341 316. 63 pp. MF–01; PC
not available EDRS.

Carter, T., and R. Segura. 1979. *Mexican Americans in School: A*

Decade of Change. New York: College Entrance Examination
Board. ED 173 003. 442 pp. MF–01; PC not available EDRS.

Casanova, U., and A. Budd. 1989. *Oral Histories of Latino Academics:
Work in Progress.* ED 310 716. 30 pp. MF–01; PC–02.

Casas, J., and J. Ponterotto. 1984. "Profiling an Invisible Minority in
Higher Education: The Chicana." *Personnel and Guidance Journal*
62: 349–53.

Chacon, M. 1982. *Chicanas in Postsecondary Education.* Stanford,
Calif.: Stanford Univ., Center for Research on Women.

Chacon, M., E. Cohen, and S. Strover. 1986. "Chicanas and Chicanos:
Barriers to Progress in Higher Education." In *Latino College Students,* edited by M. Olivas. New York: Teachers College Press.

Chankler, J., and J. Plokos. 1969. "Spanish-speaking Pupils Classified
as Educable Mentally Retarded." *Integrated Education* 7: 28–33.

Chapa, J., and R. Valencia. 1993. "Latino Population Growth, Demographic Characteristics, and Educational Stagnation: An Examination of Recent Trends." *Hispanic Journal of Behavioral Sciences*
15: 165–87.

Chavez, S. 1986. "Ethnic Minorities in Higher Education Adapting
to a New Social System." *International Journal for the Advancement of Counselling* 9: 381–84.

Chicano Coordinating Council on Higher Education. 1969. *El Plan
de Santa Barbara: A Chicano Plan for Higher Education.* Oakland,
Calif.: La Causa Publications.

Chicano/Latino Consortium. 1988. *A Report on the Status of Chica-
nos/Latinos at the University of California.* Oakland: Univ. of California, Office of the President.

Chicano Studies Development Committee. 1991. *Proposed Chicano
Studies Program at Arizona State University.* Tempe: Arizona State
Univ., Hispanic Research Center.

Collison, M. 18 March 1992. "Many Colleges Report Increase in Applications for Next Fall." *Chronicle of Higher Education:* A1+.

Colorado Association of Chicanos in Higher Education. 1983. *The
Challenge of the Future: Trends and Strategies for the Next Five
Years.* Denver: Metropolitan State College.

Colorado Commission on Higher Education. 1993. *Status of Diversity
in Colorado Public Higher Education, FY 1985–86 through
FY 1990–91.* Denver: Author. ED 351 938. 129 pp. MF–01;
PC–06.

Committee on Education and Labor. 1984. "Hearings on the Reau-
thorization of the Higher Education Act before the Subcommittee
on Postsecondary Education." Washington, D.C.: U.S. Government
Printing Office. ED 254 144. 1,493 pp. MF–12; PC–60.

Cortese, A. 1985. "The Denial of Access: Chicanos in Higher Education." *Cornell Journal of Social Relations* 18: 28–39.

———. 1992a. "Academic Achievement in Mexican Americans: Socio-
legal and Cultural Factors." *Latino Studies Journal* 3: 31–47.

————. 1992b. "Affirmative Action: Are White Women Gaining at the Expense of Black Men?" *Equity and Excellence* 25: 77–89.

Cota-Robles, E. 1992. "Institutional Policy and Practice in Doctoral Graduate Student Affirmative Action." In *Minorities in Graduate Education,* edited by J. Jones, M. Goertz, and C. Kuh. Princeton, N.J.: Educational Testing Service.

Cross, K., and E. Fideler. 1989. "Community College Missions: Priorities in the Mid-1980s." *Journal of Higher Education* 60: 209–16.

Cuadraz, G. 1989. "Experiences of Multiple Marginality: A Case Study of Chicana 'Scholarship Women.'" Paper presented at an annual meeting of the Sociologists for Women in Society, San Francisco, California.

de la Puente, M. 1992. "The Census Undercount of the Hispanic Population." *Latino Studies Journal* 3: 67–81.

Delgado, R. 1988. *Minority Law Professors' Lives: The Bell-Delgado Survey.* Working Papers Series 3. Madison: Univ. of Wisconsin–Madison, Law School Institute for Legal Studies.

————. 1991. "Affirmative Action as a Majoritarian Device: Or, Do You Really Want to Be a Role Model?" *Michigan Law Review* 89: 1221–31.

de los Santos, A. 1976. "Emerging Chicano Administrators in Higher Education." *Emergent Leadership* 1: 1/–19.

————. 1978. *Hispanics in the Community/Junior Colleges: Donde Estamos en al Ano 1978.* ED 180 509. 37 pp. MF–01; PC 02.

————. 1984. "The Connection between Postsecondary Programs for Hispanics and Elementary and Secondary Schools." In *Equality Postponed: Continuing Barriers to Higher Education in the 1980s,* edited by S. Adolphus. New York: College Entrance Examination Board.

de los Santos, A., J. Montemayor, and E. Solis. 1983. "Chicano Students in Institutions of Higher Education: Access, Attrition, and Achievement." *Aztlan* 14: 79–110.

De Necochea, G. 1988. "Expanding the Hispanic College Pool: Precollege Strategies that Work." *Change* 20: 61–62.

Duran, R. 1983. *Hispanics' Education and Background.* New York: College Entrance Examination Board. ED 230 665. 162 pp. MF–01; PC not available EDRS.

————. 1986. "Prediction of Hispanics' College Achievement." In *Latino College Students,* edited by M. Olivas. New York: Teachers College Press.

————. Forthcoming. "Hispanic Student Achievement." In *Minorities in Higher Education,* edited by M. Justiz and L. Bjork. New York: Macmillan.

Duster, T. 1976. "The Structure of Privilege and Its Universe of Discourse." *American Sociologist* 11: 73–78.

Easterlin, R. 1989. "Demography Is Not Destiny in Higher Education." In *Shaping Higher Education's Future,* edited by A. Levine and

Associates. San Francisco: Jossey-Bass.

Eastland, T., and W. Bennett. 1979. *Counting by Race: Equality from the Founding Fathers to Bakke and Weber.* New York: Basic Books.

Eaton, J. 1988. "Minorities, Transfer, and Higher Education." *Peabody Journal of Education* 66: 58–70.

———. 1991. "The Many Faces of Transfer Education." *New Directions for Community Colleges* 19: 77–86.

Ekstrom, R., M. Goertz, J. Pollack, and D. Rock. 1987. "Who Drops Out of High School and Why? Findings from a National Study." In *School Dropouts: Patterns and Policies,* edited by G. Natriello. New York: Teachers College Press.

England, P., K. Meier, and L. Fraga. 1988. "Barriers to Equal Opportunity: Educational Practices and Minority Students." *Urban Affairs Quarterly* 23: 635–46.

Escobedo, T. 1980. "Are Hispanic Women in Higher Education the Nonexistent Minority?" *Educational Researcher* 9: 7–12.

Espinosa, R., and A. Ochoa. 1986. "Concentration of California Hispanic Students in Schools with Low Achievement: A Research Note." *American Journal of Education* 95: 77–95.

Esquibel, A. 1977. "The Chicano Administrator in Colleges and Universities of the Southwest." Doctoral dissertation, Univ. of New Mexico.

Estrada, L. 1988. "Anticipating the Demographic Future." *Change* 20: 14–19.

Evangelauf, J. 20 January 1993. "Number of Minority Students in Colleges Rose by 9% from 1990 to 1991, U.S. Reports." *Chronicle of Higher Education:* A30–A31.

Exum, W. 1983. "Climbing the Crystal Stair: Values, Affirmative Action, and Minority Faculty." *Social Problems* 30: 383–99.

Fernandez, R., and G. Shu. 1988. "School Dropouts: New Approaches to an Enduring Problem." *Education and Urban Society* 20: 363–86.

Fiske, E. 1988. "The Undergraduate Hispanic Experience: A Case of Juggling Two Cultures." *Change* 20: 29–33.

Frances, C. 1989. "Uses and Misuses of Demographic Projections: Lessons for the 1990s." In *Shaping Higher Education's Future,* edited by A. Levine and Associates. San Francisco: Jossey-Bass.

Frazier, D., and R. DeBlassie. 1982. "A Comparison of Self-Concept in Mexican American and Non–Mexican American Late Adolescents." *Adolescence* 17: 327–34.

Gandara, P. 1980. "Chicano Scholars: Against All Odds." ED 207 743. 12 pp. MF–01; PC not available EDRS.

———. 1982. "Passing through the Eye of the Needle: High Achieving Chicanas." *Hispanic Journal of Behavioral Sciences* 4: 167–80.

———. 1986. "Chicanos in Higher Education: The Politics of Self-Interest." *American Journal of Education* 95: 256–72.

Garcia, A. 1986. "Studying Chicanas: Bringing Women into the Frame of Chicano Studies." In *Chicana Voices: Intersections of Class, Race, and Gender,* edited by T. Cordova, N. Cantu, G. Cardenas, J. Garcia, and C. Sierra. Austin: Univ. of Texas at Austin, Center for Mexican American Studies.

Garcia, E. 1978. "Joint Faculty Appointments: An Administrative Dilemma in Chicano Studies." *Explorations in Ethnic Studies* 2: 1–8.

Garcia, R. 1980. *Educational Hierarchies and Social Differentiation: The Structural Patterns of Chicano Participation in Colleges and Universities in the Southwest, 1972–1976.* ED 201 294. 113 pp. MF–01; PC–05.

Garza, H. 1988. "The 'Barrioization' of Hispanic Faculty." *Educational Record* 68/69: 122–24.

———. 1989. "Second Class Academics: Chicano/Latino Faculty in U.S. Universities." Fresno: California State Univ. at Fresno, Dept. of Chicano and Latin American Studies.

———. 1991. "Academic Power, Discourse, and Legitimacy: Minority Scholars in U.S. Universities." Fresno: California State Univ. at Fresno, Dept. of Chicano and Latin American Studies.

———. 1992. "Origins and Evolution of an Alternative Scholarship and Scholarly Organization." In *Chicano Discourse: Selected Conference Proceedings of the National Association for Chicano Studies,* edited by T. Mindiola and E. Zamora. Houston: Univ. of Houston, Mexican American Studies Program.

Ginsberg, R., and A. Bennett. 1989. "Reform Initiatives and Minorities in Higher Education." *Education and Urban Society* 21: 245–59.

Golladay, M. 1989. "Women and Minority Faculty in Engineering: Reviewing the Figures." *Engineering Education* 79: 573–76.

Gomez Quinones, J. 1978. *Mexican Students por la Raza: The Chicano Student Movement in Southern California, 1967–1977.* Santa Barbara: La Raza Publications.

Gonzalez, G. 1982. *Progressive Education: A Marxist Interpretation.* Studies in Marxism, vol. 8. Minneapolis: Marxist Educational Press.

———. 1990. *Chicano Education in the Era of Segregation.* Philadelphia: Balch Institute Press.

Grant, J., and R. Goldsmith. 1979. *Bilingual Education and Federal Law: An Overview.* Austin: Dissemination and Assessment Center for Bilingual Education.

Griffith, J., M. Frase, and J. Ralph. 1989. "American Education: The Challenge of Change." *Population Bulletin* 44: 4.

Grubb, W. 1991. "The Decline of Community College Transfer Rates." *Journal of Higher Education* 62: 194–222.

Halcon, J., and M. de la Luz Reyes. 1991. " 'Trickle-Down' Reform: Hispanics, Higher Education, and the Excellence Movement." *Urban Review* 23: 117–35.

Hamilton, I. 1973. *Graduate School Programs for Minority/Disadvantaged Students: Report of an Initial Survey.* Princeton, N.J.:

Educational Testing Service. ED 081 304. 110 pp. MF–01; PC–05.

Haro, C. 1977a. *Mexicano/Chicano Concerns and School Desegregation in Los Angeles.* Los Angeles: Univ. of California at Los Angeles, Chicano Studies Center Publications.

————. 1977b. "Truant and Low-Achieving Chicano Student Perceptions in the High School Social System." *Aztlan* 8: 99–131.

Haro, R. 1989. "Hispanics and California Public Universities: Challenges and Opportunities." *LA RED/The Net: The Hispanic Journal of Education, Commentary, and Reviews* 2: 7–11.

Hayden, T. 30 June 1993. "Amid Clash Crisis, Hispanics Win a Historic Victory." *Chronicle of Higher Education:* A40.

Hayes-Bautista, D., W. Schink, and J. Chapa. 1988. *The Burden of Support: Young Latinos in an Aging Society.* Stanford, Calif.: Stanford Univ. Press.

Hiramo-Nakamishi, M. 1986. "The Extent and Relevance of Pre–High School Attrition and Delayed Education for Hispanics." *Hispanic Journal of Behavioral Sciences* 8: 61–76.

Hu-Dehart, E. 1983. "Women, Minorities, and Academic Freedom." In *Regulating the Intellectuals: Perspectives on Academic Freedom in the 1980s,* edited by C. Kaplan and E. Schrecker. New York: Praeger.

Humphreys, L. 1988. "Trends in Levels of Academic Achievement of Blacks and Other Minorities." *Intelligence* 12: 231–60.

Hyland, C. 1992. "Rising Hispanic Enrollments: A New Challenge for Public Schools." In *Who Pays for Student Diversity: Population Changes and Educational Policy,* edited by J. Ward and P. Anthony. Newbury Park, Calif.: Corwin Press.

Isaac, A. 1973. "The Development and Status of Black and Brown Studies at the Claremont Colleges: The University of California at Riverside; California State College at San Bernardino; San Bernardino Valley Community College; and University College/Johnston College in Redlands, 1967–1972. A Cross Comparison." Doctoral dissertation, Claremont Graduate School.

Jackson, G. 1990. "Financial Aid, College Entry, and Affirmative Action." *American Journal of Education* 98: 523–50.

Karabel, J. 1972. "Community Colleges and Social Stratification." *Harvard Educational Review* 42: 521–62.

Katsinas, S. 1984. "Hispanic Students and Staffing Patterns in Community Colleges." ED 248 904. 17 pp. MF–01; PC–01.

Kerr, C. 1991. "International Learning and National Purposes in Higher Education." *American Behavioral Scientist* 35: 17–42.

Klor de Alva, J. 1992. "Statement by the Ad Hoc Latino GRE/MGE Conference Group." In *Minorities in Graduate Education,* edited by J. Jones, M. Goertz, and C. Kuh. Princeton, N.J.: Educational Testing Service.

Lang, M., and C. Ford. 1990. "From Access to Retention: Minority Students in Higher Education." In *Politics and Policy in the Age of Education,* edited by L. Marcus and B. Stickney. Springfield, Ill.: Charles C. Thomas.

Leal, A., and C. Monjivar. 1992. "Xenophobia or Xenophilia: Hispanic Women in Higher Education." In *Perspectives on Minority Women in Higher Education,* edited by L. Welch. New York: Praeger.

Leibowitz, A. 1980. *The Bilingual Education Act: A Legislative Analysis.* Rosslyn, Va.: National Clearinghouse for Bilingual Education.

Leon, D. 1980–81. "Racism in the University: The Case of the Educational Opportunity Program." *Humboldt Journal of Social Relations* 8: 83–101.

Leon, D., and D. McNeill. 1985. "The Fifth Class: A 19th Century Forerunner of Affirmative Action." *California History* 64: 52–57.

Levine, A. 1989. "Conclusions and Recommendations: Creating a Brighter Educational Future." In *Shaping Higher Education's Future,* edited by A. Levine and Associates. San Francisco: Jossey-Bass.

Livingston, J. 1979. *Fair Game? Inequality and Affirmative Action.* San Francisco: W.H. Freeman & Co.

Lopez, A., and R. Schultz. 1980. "Role Conflict of Chicano Administrators in Community Colleges." *Community College Review* 7: 50–55.

Lopez, R., A. Madrid-Barela, and R. Macias. 1976. *Chicanos in Higher Education: Status and Issues.* Monograph No. 7. Los Angeles: Univ. of California at Los Angeles, Chicano Studies Center. ED 136 984. 220 pp. MF–01; PC not available EDRS.

Lopez, T. 1991. *Some African-American and Hispanic Voices from the University of Toledo (Ohio).* ED 328 153. 53 pp. MF–01; PC–03.

Lunneborg, C., and P. Lunneborg. 1986. "Beyond Prediction: The Challenge of Minority Achievement in Higher Education." *Journal of Multicultural Counseling and Development* 14: 77–84.

McKevitt, G. 1990–91. "Hispanic Californians and Catholic Higher Education: The Diary of Jesus Maria Estudillo, 1857–1864." *California History* 69: 320–31.

Madrid, A. 1982. "Overcoming the 'Only' Phenomenon: The Continuing Struggle of Chicanos and Puerto Ricans to Improve Their Professional Status in Institutions of Higher Education." In *Hispanics in Higher Education: Leadership and Vision for the Next 25 Years,* edited by L. Valverde and S. Garcia. Austin: Univ. of Texas at Austin, Office for Advanced Research in Hispanic Education.

———. 1988. "Missing People and Others." *Change* 20: 55–59.

Manuel, H. 1965. *Spanish-Speaking Children of the Southwest: Their Education and Welfare.* Austin: Univ. of Texas Press.

Martinez, R. 1986. *Minority Youth Dropouts: Personal, Social, and Institutional Reasons for Leaving School.* ED 280 934. 48 pp. MF–01; PC–02.

———. 1990. "Ethnic Studies: Past, Present and Future." Paper presented at the Diversity of Excellence and the Excellence of Diversity Conference, Univ. of Colorado at Denver.

———. 1991. "The Politics of Ethnicity in Social Science." In *The Estate of Social Knowledge,* edited by J. Brown and D. van Keuren. Baltimore: Johns Hopkins Univ. Press.

Martinez, R., A. Hernandez, and A. Aguirre, Jr. Forthcoming. "Latino Faculty Attitudes toward the Workplace." *Journal of the Mexican American Association of Educators.*

Medina, M. 1988. "Hispanic Apartheid in American Public Education." *Educational Administration Quarterly* 24: 336–49.

Melendez, S., and J. Petrovich. 1989. "Hispanic Women Students in Higher Education: Meeting the Challenge of Diversity." In *Educating The Majority: Women Challenge Tradition in Higher Education,* edited by C. Pearson, D. Shavlik, and J. Touchton. New York: Macmillan.

Menchaca, M., and R. Valencia. 1990. "Anglo-Saxon Ideologies in the 1920s–1930s: Their Impact on the Segregation of Mexican Students in California." *Anthropology and Education Quarterly* 21: 222–49.

Milem, J., and H. Astin. 1993. "The Changing Composition of the Faculty: What Does It Really Mean for Diversity?" *Change* 25: 21–27.

Monsivais, G. 1990. "Policy Issue: The Attrition of Latino Teachers." Claremont, Calif.: Tomas Rivera Center.

Muñoz, C. 1984. "The Development of Chicano Studies, 1968–1981." In *Chicano Studies: A Multidisciplinary Approach,* edited by E. Garcia, F. Lomeli, and I. Ortiz. New York: Teachers College Press.

———. 1989. *Youth, Identity, Power: The Chicano Movement.* New York: Verso.

National Center for Education Statistics. 1991a. *Digest of Education Statistics, 1990.* NCES91-660. Washington, D.C.: U.S. Government Printing Office. ED 330 086. 526 pp. MF–02; PC–22.

———. 1991b. *Digest of Education Statistics, 1991.* Washington, D.C.: U.S. Government Printing Office. ED 340 141. 540 pp. MF–02; PC–22.

———. 1991c. "National Higher Education Statistics: Fall 1991." Washington, D.C.: U.S. Government Printing Office. ED 340 314. 22 pp. MF–01; PC–01.

———. 1991d. *Projections of Education Statistics to 2002.* Washington, D.C.: U.S. Government Printing Office. ED 341 697. 229 pp. MF–01; PC–10.

———. 1992a. *The Condition of Education, 1992.* Washington, D.C.: U.S. Government Printing Office. ED 344 347. 446 pp. MF–01; PC–18.

———. 1992b. *Trends in Racial/Ethnic Enrollment in Higher Education: Fall 1980 through Fall 1990.* Washington, D.C.: U.S. Department of Education.

National Research Council. 1981. *Young and Senior Science and Engineering Faculty.* Washington, D.C.: National Science Foundation. ED 222 375. 193 pp. MF–01; PC not available EDRS.

National Science Foundation. 1989. *Research Participation and Characteristics of Science and Engineering Faculty.* Washington, D.C.: Author.

Negrete, L. 1981. "The Education of Mexican Students in the United States." *Campo Libre* 1: 35–84.

Nettles, M. 1990. *Black, Hispanic, and White Doctoral Students: Before, During, and After Enrolling in Graduate Education School.* Princeton, N.J.: Educational Testing Service, Minority Graduate Education Project.

———. 1992. "Black, Hispanic, and White Doctoral Students: Before, During, and After Enrolling in Graduate Education. A Summary Report." In *Minorities in Graduate Education,* edited by J. Jones, M. Goertz, and C. Kuh. Princeton, N.J.: Educational Testing Service.

Nieves-Squires, S. 1991. "Hispanic Women: Making Their Presence on Campus Less Tenuous." Washington, D.C.: Association of American Colleges, Project on the Status and Education of Women. ED 334 907. 16 pp. MF–01; PC–01.

———. 1992. "Hispanic Women in the U.S. Academic Context." In *Perspectives on Minority Women in Higher Education,* edited by L. Welch. New York: Praeger.

Nora, A. 1990. "Campus-Based Aid Programs as Determinants of Retention among Hispanic Community College Students." *Journal of Higher Education* 61: 312–31.

Nora, A., and F. Horvath. 1989. "Financial Assistance: Minority Enrollments and Persistence." *Education and Urban Society* 21: 299–311.

Nuñez, R., and R. Contreras. 1992. "Principles and Foundations of Chicano Studies: Chicano Organization on University Campuses in California." In *Chicano Discourse: Selected Conference Proceedings of the National Association for Chicano Studies,* edited by T. Mindiola and E. Zamora. Houston: Univ. of Houston, Mexican American Studies Program.

Oakes, J. 1985. *Keeping Track: How Schools Structure Inequality.* New Haven: Yale Univ. Press.

———. 1986a. "Keeping Track, Part 1: The Policy and Practice of Curriculum Inequality." *Phi Delta Kappan* 68: 12–18.

———. 1986b. "Keeping Track, Part 2: The Policy and Practice of Curriculum Inequality." *Phi Delta Kappan* 68: 148–54.

Olivas, M. 1979. *The Dilemma of Access: Minorities in Two-Year Colleges.* Washington, D.C.: Howard Univ. Press.

———. 1981. *Financial Aid: Access and Packaging Policies.* Stanford, Calif.: Stanford Univ., Institute for Research on Educational Finance and Governance.

———. 1982. "Federal Higher Education Policy: The Case of His-

panics." *Educational Evaluation and Policy Analysis* 4: 301–10.
———. 1984. "New Populations, New Arrangements." In *Equality Postponed: Continuing Barriers to Higher Education in the 1980s,* edited by S. Adolphus. New York: College Entrance Examination Board.
———. 1985. "Financial Aid Packaging Policies: Access and Ideology." *Journal of Higher Education* 56: 462–75.
———. 1986a. "Financial Aid for Hispanics: Access, Ideology, and Packaging Policies." In *Latino College Students,* edited by M. Olivas. New York: Teachers College Press.
———. 1986b. "Introduction. Research on Latino College Students: A Theoretical Framework and Inquiry." In *Latino College Students,* edited by M. Olivas. New York: Teachers College Press.
———. 1988. "Latino Faculty at the Border." *Change* 20: 6–9.
———. 1992. "Trout Fishing in Catfish Ponds." In *Minorities in Graduate Education,* edited by J. Jones, M. Goertz, and C. Kuh. Princeton, N.J.: Educational Testing Service.
O'Malley, J. 1987. *Academic Growth of High School–Age Hispanic Students in America.* Washington, D.C.: National Center for Education Statistics. ED 281 918. 142 pp. MF–01; PC–06.
Orfield, G. 1989. "Hispanics." In *Shaping Higher Education's Future,* edited by A. Levine and Associates. San Francisco: Jossey-Bass.
Orfield, G., F. Montfort, and R. George. 1987. *School Segregation in the 1980s: Trends in Metropolitan Areas.* Washington, D.C.: Joint Center for Political Studies. ED 285 946. 56 pp. MF–01; PC–03.
Orozco, C. 1986. "Sexism in Chicano Studies and the Community." In *Chicana Voices: Intersections of Class, Race, and Gender,* edited by T. Cordova, N. Cantu, G. Cardenas, J. Garcia, and C. Sierra. Austin: Univ. of Texas at Austin, Mexican American Studies Center.
Ortego y Gasca, P. 1975. "On Prejudice and Discrimination." *La Luz* 4: 12.
Ortiz, V. 1986. "Generational Status, Family Background, and Educational Attainment among Hispanic Youth and non-Hispanic White Youth." In *Latino College Students,* edited by M. Olivas. New York: Teachers College Press.
Orum, L. 1986. *The Education of Hispanics: Status and Implications.* Washington, D.C.: National Council of La Raza.
Padilla, R. 1987. "Chicano Studies Revisited: Still in Search of the Campus and the Community." In *A Symposium on Chicano Studies,* edited by A. Gonzalez and D. Sandoval. Los Angeles: National Association for Chicano Studies.
Paredes, R. 1991. "Chicano Studies at UCLA: A Controversy with National Implications." *Hispanic Outlook in Higher Education* 2: 10–11.
Payan, R., R. Peterson, and N. Castille. 1984. *Access to College for Mexican Americans in the Southwest: Replication after 10 Years.* Report No. 84-3. New York: College Entrance Examination Board.

ED 250 978. 40 pp. MF–01; PC not available EDRS.

Pennock-Roman, M. 1988. *The Status of Research on the Scholastic Aptitude Test (SAT) and Hispanic Students in Postsecondary Education*. Princeton, N.J.: Educational Testing Service.

Phillips, W., and R. Blumberg. 1983. "Tokenism and Organizational Change." *Integrated Education* 20: 34–39.

Pincus, P., and S. DeCamp. 1989. "Minority Community College Students Who Transfer to Four-Year Colleges: A Study of a Matched Sample of B.A. Recipients and Nonrecipients." *Community/Junior College* 13: 191–219.

Plastino, A. 1979. "The Legal Status of Bilingual Education in America's Public Schools." *Duquesne Law Review* 17: 473–505.

Rendon, L. 1986. "A Comprehensive Strategy to Examine and Address Transfer Education." ED 270 191. 23 pp. MF–01; PC–01.

Rendon, L., M. Justiz, and P. Resta. 1988. *Transfer Education in Southwest Border Community Colleges.* ED 296 748. 304 pp. MF–01; PC–13.

Rendon, L., and Nora, A. 1988. *Salvaging Minority Transfer Students: Toward New Policies that Facilitate Baccalaureate Attainment.* ED 305 098. 39 pp. MF–01; PC–02.

————. 1989. "A Synthesis and Application of Research on Hispanic Students in Community Colleges." *Community College Review* 17: 17 24.

Reyes, M. de la Luz, and J. Halcon. 1988. "Racism in Academia: The Old Wolf Revisited." *Harvard Educational Review* 58: 299 315.

————. 1991. "Practices of the Academy: Barriers to Access for Chicano Academics." In *The Racial Crisis in American Higher Education,* edited by P. Altbach and K. Lomotey. Albany: State University of New York Press.

Rivera, J., and L. Burrola. 1984. "Chicano Studies Programs in Higher Education: Scenarios for Future Research." *Aztlan* 15: 277–93.

Rivera, M. 1985. "El Cedazo: Sifting and Shifting or the Hispanic Participation in the Management of the California Community Colleges, 1973–83." Paper presented at an annual conference of the Texas Association of Chicanos in Higher Education, McAllen, Texas. ED 274 469. 44 pp. MF–01; PC not available EDRS.

Rivera, T. 1982. "The Role of the Chicano Academic and the Chicano Nonacademic Community." In *Hispanics in Higher Education: Leadership and Vision for the Next 25 Years,* edited by L. Valverde and S. Garcia. Austin: Univ. of Texas at Austin, Office for Advanced Research in Hispanic Education.

Rochin, R. 1972. "The Short and Turbulent Life of Chicano Studies: A Preliminary Study of Emerging Programs and Problems." *Social Science Quarterly* 53: 884–94.

Rochin, R., and de la Torre, A. 1986. *The Current Status and Future of Chicano Studies Programs: Are They Academically Sound?* ED 273 429. 34 pp. MF–01; PC–02.

————. 1988. "Strengthening Chicano Studies Programs." *LA RED/ The Net* 1: 11–30.

Rodriguez, R. 1993. "Battle over UCLA's Chicano Studies Program Ends." *Black Issues in Higher Education* 10: 26–27.

Romero, D. 1977. "The Impact and Use of Minority Faculty within a University." Paper presented at an annual meeting of the American Psychological Association, San Francisco, California.

Rosaldo, R. 1985. *Chicano Studies, 1970–1984.* Working Paper No. 10. Stanford, Calif.: Stanford Univ., Center for Chicano Research.

Rosenblum, G., and B. Rosenblum. 1990. "Segmented Labor Markets in Institutions of Higher Learning." *Sociology of Education* 63: 151–64.

St. John, E., and J. Noell. 1989. "The Effects of Student Financial Aid on Access to Higher Education: An Analysis of Progress with Special Consideration of Minority Enrollment." *Research in Higher Education* 30: 563–81.

Sanchez, A. 1974. "Chicano Student Movement at San Jose State." In *Parameters of Institutional Change: Chicano Experiences in Education,* edited by the Southwest Network. Hayward, Calif.: World Publications.

San Miguel, G. 1987. *"Let All of Them Take Heed": Mexican Americans and the Campaign for Educational Equality in Texas, 1910–1981.* Austin: Univ. of Texas Press.

Sazama, G. 1992. "Has Federal Student Aid Contributed to Equality in Higher Education?" *American Journal of Economics and Sociology* 51: 129–46.

Schwartz, A. 1989. "Middle-Class Educational Values among Latino Gang Members in East Los Angeles County High Schools." *Urban Education* 24: 323–42.

Serrata, A. 1987. "An Organizational History of Chicano Studies Research Center, UCLA, 1969–1985." Los Angeles: Univ. of California at Los Angeles, Dept. of Sociology.

Simoniella, K. 1981. "On Investigating the Attitudes toward Achievement and Success in Eight Professional U.S. Mexican Women." *Aztlan* 12: 121–37.

Smith, C., and V. Hixson. 1987. "The Work of University Professors: Evidence of Segmented Labor Markets inside the Academy." *Current Research on Occupations and Professions* 4: 159–80.

Smith, E., and S. Witt. 1990. "Black Faculty and Affirmative Action at Predominantly White Institutions." *Western Journal of Black Studies* 14: 9–16.

Smith, P. 1990. *Killing the Spirit: Higher Education in America.* New York: Viking Press.

Sorensen, A., and M. Hallinan. 1986. "Effects of Ability Grouping on Growth in Academic Achievement." *American Educational Research Journal* 23: 519–42.

Sotello, C., and V. Turner. 1992. "It Takes Two to Transfer: Relational

Networks and Educational Outcomes." *Community College Review* 19: 27–33.

Sowell, T. 1980. " *Weber* and *Bakke,* and the Presuppositions of 'Affirmative Action.'" *Wayne Law Review* 26: 1309–36.

Stampen, J., and A. Cabrera. 1988. "The Targeting and Packaging of Student Aid and Its Effect on Attrition." *Economics of Education Review* 7: 29–46.

Steinberg, L., P. Blinde, and K. Chan. 1984. "Dropping Out among Language Minority Youth." *Review of Educational Research* 54: 113–32.

Stewart, J. 2 June 1993. "Earned Degrees Conferred by U.S. Institutions, 1990–91." *Chronicle of Higher Education:* A25.

Suzuki, B. 1989. "Asians." In *Shaping Higher Education's Future,* edited by A. Levine and Associates. San Francisco: Jossey Bass.

Terzian, A. 1991. "A Model in Community College Transfer Programs." *New Directions for Community Colleges* 19: 87–92.

Thomas, G. 1992. "Participation and Degree Attainment of African-American and Latino Students in Graduate Education Relative to Other Racial and Ethnic Groups: An Update from Office of Civil Rights Data." *Harvard Educational Review* 62: 45–65.

Thomas, G., and D. Hirsch. 1989. "Blacks." In *Shaping Higher Education's Future,* edited by A. Levine and Associates. San Francisco: Jossey-Bass.

Thornburg, H. 1974. "An Investigation of a Dropout Program among Arizona's Minority Youth." *Education* 94: 249–65.

Thornburg, H., and R. Grinder. 1975. "Children of Aztlan: The Mexican American Experience." In *Youth* (The Seventy-fourth Yearbook of the National Society for the Study of Education), edited by R. Havighurst and P. Dreyer. Chicago: Univ. of Chicago Press.

Trent, W. 1991. "Student Affirmative Action in Higher Education: Addressing Underrepresentation." In *The Racial Crisis in American Higher Education,* edited by P. Altbach and K. Lomotey. Albany: State Univ. of New York Press.

Trow, M. 1992. "Class, Race, and Higher Education in America." *American Behavioral Scientist* 35: 585–605.

Trueba, H. 1990. "Mainstream and Minority Cultures: A Chicano Perspective." In *The American Cultural Dialogue and Its Transmission,* edited by G. Spindler and L. Spindler. New York: Falmer Press.

———. 1993. "Race and Ethnicity: The Role of Universities in Healing Multicultural America." *Educational Theory* 43: 41–54.

UCLA News. 7 June 1993. "Strengthened Plan for Interdisciplinary Programs Created by UCLA Administration and Faculty: Chicana and Chicano Studies Program to Be First Center for Interdisciplinary Instruction and Named in Honor of Cesar Chavez." Press release.

Ulibarri, H. 1972. "The Bicultural Myth and the Education of the Mexican American." *Journal of Comparative Cultures* 1: 83–95.

U.S. Bureau of the Census. 1963. "Persons of Spanish Surname, 1960." PC2-1B. Washington, D.C.: U.S. Government Printing Office.

———. 1973. "Persons of Spanish Surname, 1970." PC2-10. Washington, D.C.: U.S. Government Printing Office.

———. 1976. "Persons of Spanish Origin in the United States, March 1975." P-20-290. Washington, D.C.: U.S. Government Printing Office. ED 110 255. 10 pp. MF–01; PC–01.

———. 1982. "Persons of Spanish Origin by State, 1980." PC80-S1-7. Washington, D.C.: U.S. Government Printing Office.

———. 1985. "Persons of Spanish Origin in the United States, March 1985." P-20-403. Washington, D.C.: U.S. Government Printing Office. ED 266 224. 8 pp. MF–01; PC–01.

———. 1989. "The Hispanic Population in the United States, March 1988." P-20-438. Washington, D.C.: U.S. Government Printing Office.

———. 1991a. *The Black Population in the United States, March 1990 and 1989.* P-20-448. Washington, D.C.: U.S. Government Printing Office. ED 341 750. 148 pp. MF–01; PC–06.

———. 1991b. *The Hispanic Population in the United States, March 1990.* P-20-449. Washington, D.C.: U.S. Government Printing Office. ED 342 872. 50 pp. MF–01; PC–02.

———. 1991c. *The Hispanic Population of the U.S. Southwest Borderland.* P-23-172. Washington, D.C.: U.S. Government Printing Office.

———. 1991d. "Race and Hispanic Origin." 1990 Census Profile No. 2. Washington, D.C.: U.S. Government Printing Office. ED 346 228. 9 pp. MF–01; PC–01.

———. 1992. *The Asian and Pacific Islander Population in the United States, March 1991 and 1990.* P-20-459. Washington, D.C.: U.S. Government Printing Office. ED 351 434. 110 pp. MF–01; PC–05.

U.S. Commission on Civil Rights. 1971. *Ethnic Isolation of Mexican Americans in the Public Schools of the Southwest.* Washington, D.C.: U.S. Government Printing Office. ED 052 849. 97 pp. MF–01; PC–04.

———. 1972. *The Excluded Student: Educational Practices Affecting Mexican Americans in the Southwest.* Report 3. Washington, D.C.: U.S. Government Printing Office. ED 062 069. 77 pp. MF–01; PC–04.

———. 1977. *The State of Civil Rights, 1976.* Washington, D.C.: U.S. Government Printing Office. ED 137 157. 43 pp. MF–01; PC–02.

U.S. Dept. of Health and Human Services. 1985. *Location Patterns of Minority and Other Health Professionals.* HRS-P-OD85-2. Washington, D.C.: Author. ED 265 051. 88 pp. MF–01; PC–04.

Univ. of California. 1985. *University of California Undergraduate Student Affirmative Action Five-Year Plan.* Berkeley: Univ. of California, Office of the President.

Univ. of Colorado, Faculty Senate Minority Affairs Committee. 1987. *Minorities and Strategic Planning at the University of Colorado.* Boulder: Univ. of Colorado, Office of the Associate Vice President for Human Resources.

Uribe, O., and R. Verdugo. 1990. "A Research Note on the Status and Working Conditions of Hispanic Faculty." Paper presented at an annual meeting of the American Educational Research Association, Boston, Massachusetts.

Usdan, M. 1984. "New Trends in Urban Demography." *Education and Urban Society* 16: 399–414.

Valdivieso, R. 1986. *Must They Wait Another Generation? Hispanics and Secondary School Reform.* ED 273 705. 59 pp. MF–01; PC–03.

Valencia, R. 1984. *Understanding School Closures: Discriminatory Impact on Chicano and Black Students.* Monograph Series No. 1. Stanford, Calif,; Stanford Univ., Center for Chicano Research Policy. ED 271 251. 142 pp. MF–01; PC–06.

Valverde, L. 1975. "Prohibitive Trends in Chicano Faculty Employment." In *Chicanos in Higher Education,* edited by H. Casso and G. Roman. Albuquerque: Univ. of New Mexico Press.

———. 1981. "Achieving Equity in Higher Education: Inclusion and Retention of Hispanic Academics." In *Education and Chicanos: Issues and Research,* edited by T. Escobedo. Monograph No. 8. Los Angeles: Univ. of California at Los Angeles, Spanish Speaking Mental Health Research Center.

———. 1988, "The Missing Element: Hispanics at the Top in Higher Education." *Change* 20: 11.

Valverde, L., and E. Ramirez. 1977. "Chicano Professionals in Texas Higher Education: A Statistical Summary." *El Cuaderno* 1: 26–30.

Valverde, S. 1987. "A Comparative Study of Hispanic High School Dropouts and Graduates: Why Do Some Leave School Early and Some Finish?" *Education and Urban Society* 19: 320–29.

Vasquez, M. 1982. "Confronting Barriers to the Participation of Mexican American Women in Higher Education." *Hispanic Journal of Behavioral Sciences* 4: 147–65.

Velez, W., and R. Javalgi. 1987. "Two-Year College to Four-Year College: The Likelihood of Transfer." *American Journal of Education* 96: 81–94.

Verdugo, R. 1992. "Analysis of Tenure among Hispanic Higher Education Faculty." *AMAE Journal* (Special Edition: Chicanos in Higher Education): 23–30.

Vigil, D. 1988. "The Nexus of Class, Culture, and Gender in the Education of Mexican American Females." In *The Broken Web: The Educational Experience of Hispanic Americans,* edited by T. McKenna and F. Ortiz. Encino, Calif.: Floricanto Press.

Walsh, C. 1987. "Schooling and the Civic Exclusion of Latinos: Toward a Discourse of Dissonance." *Journal of Education* 169: 115–31.

Washburn, D. 1981. *Ethnic Studies in the United States: Higher Education.* ED 206 232. 161 pp. MF–01; PC–07.

Willie, C. 1987. "On Excellence and Equity in Higher Education." *Journal of Negro Education* 56: 485–92.

———. 1988. "Initiation of Desegregation Litigation: A Majority or Minority Responsibility." In *Desegregating America's Colleges and Universities,* edited by J. Williams. New York: Teachers College Press.

Wilson, R., and D. Carter. 1988. *Minorities in Higher Education.* Seventh Annual Status Report. ED 320 509. 58 pp. MF–01; PC–03.

Witt, S. 1990. *The Pursuit of Race and Gender Equality in American Academe.* New York: Praeger.

Young, G. 1992. "Chicana College Students on the Texas-Mexico Border: Transition and Transformation." *Hispanic Journal of Behavioral Sciences* 14: 341–52.

INDEX

A

AACHE. See Arizona Association of Chicanos for Higher Education in Arizona
ACR. See Assembly Concurrent Resolution
Affirmative action, 20-21, 67, 69
African-American, 4,12-13, 17
    financial assistance, 49
Aguirre, Adalberto Jr., xv
American Council on Education, 47
American-Mexican War of 1846 to 1848, 17
Antioch college, 36
Arizona Association of Chicanos for Higher Education in Arizona (AACHE), 23
Asian. See Asian-American
Asian-American
    average SAT scores, 13
    educational outcomes, 3-4
    enrollment increases, 48
Associate of Arts degree, 37-38
Aztlan
    El Plan Espiritual de, 18
    El Movimiento Estudiantil Chicano de (MEChA), 18

B

Bakke, Allan, 21
barrioization, 61. See also Isolation
Basic education Opportunity Grants. See Pell Grants
blacks. See African-American

C

California
    Assembly Concurrent Resolution (ACR), 21-22
    Assessment Program (CAP), 8
    education of Chicanos. See education of Chicanos.
californios, 17
CAP. See California Assessment Program
Cesar Chavez Center for Interdisciplinary Instruction, 32
Charles River ferry, xv
Chicana
    enrollment gains, 46
    ethnic identification, 55
    recipients of professional degrees, 47
Chicano
    administrators lacking, 56
    definition of term, xvii
    educational attainment compared to whites, 3-4
    educational attainment compared to Asians, 5-6
    self determination, 22

F

Fife, Jonathan D., xvi
Ford Foundation, 27, 50

G

Garza, Ray, xvii
general education requirements, 36
G.I. Bill of Rights. See Servicemen's Readjustment Act of 1944
Guaranteed Student Loan Program. See Stafford Loan Program

H

HACU. See Hispanic Association of Colleges and Universities
Harvard University, xv, 45
HEW. See U. S. Department of Health, Education and Welfare
High School and Beyond Study, 39
high school dropout rate, 5-6, 11
Higher Education
        Act of 1965, 27, 35
        Guidelines, 21
Hispanic
        Association of Colleges and Universities (HACU), 18, 50
        enrollment increases, 48-49
        includes Chicano, 15, 54-55

I

isolation, 7-9, 11, 16, 61
        continuing, 11-12
        costs, 9
IUP research forum, xvii

J

Joliet Illinois, 37
junior college. See community college

L

land grant colleges, 36
language instruction, 70
liberal education, 36
LL.M. program, 60

M

Madrid Arturo, xvii
Martinez, Ruben O., xv
masters degrees, 43, 45, 47-48
MEChA. See El Movimiento Estudiantil Chicano de Aztlan
mentors. See role model
Mexican American
        identification, 58

---

students in the 1870s, 24
Morrill Act of 1862, 36

N

NACS. See National Association for Chicano Studies
National
        Association for Chicano Studies (NACS), 18, 31
        Chicano Council on Higher Education, 57
        Collegiate Athletic Association (NCAA), 42
        Defense Education Act (NDEA), 27, 35
        Hispanic Scholarship Fund, 27
        Institute for Mental Health, 27
        Labor Relations Act of 1935, 20, 22
        Longitudinal Study of the Class of 1972, 39
Native Americans, 17
        educational achievement, 1
nativistic movements, 29
NCAA. See Collegiate Athletic Association
NDEA. See National Defense Education Act

O

OFCC. See Office of Federal Contract compliance
Office for Civil Rights, 21
Office of Federal Contract compliance (OFCC), 20
Olivas, Michael, xviii

P

Pell Grants, 27
PEW
        Foundation, 27
        manuscript project, xvii
political correctness, 29
processual initiatives, 70-71, 73-74, 76
Puerto Rican
        educational outcomes, 4
        faculty, 55

R

residential segregation, 7
reverse discrimination, 21
role model, 65-66, 71, 75-76.
Romano, Don Octavio, 30-31

S

Santa Barbara, El Plan de. See El Plan de Santa Barbara
Santa Clara college, 17
SAT, 9, 12-13
scholarship programs for minorities, 49-50

ASHE-ERIC HIGHER EDUCATION REPORTS

Since 1983, the Association for the Study of Higher Education (ASHE) and the Educational Resources Information Center (ERIC) Clearinghouse on Higher Education, a sponsored project of the School of Education and Human Development at The George Washington University, have cosponsored the *ASHE-ERIC Higher Education Report* series. The 1993 series is the twenty-second overall and the fifth to be published by the School of Education and Human Development at the George Washington University.

Each monograph is the definitive analysis of a tough higher education problem, based on thorough research of pertinent literature and institutional experiences. Topics are identified by a national survey. Noted practitioners and scholars are then commissioned to write the reports, with experts providing critical reviews of each manuscript before publication.

Eight monographs (10 before 1985) in the ASHE-ERIC Higher Education Report series are published each year and are available on individual and subscription bases. Subscription to eight issues is $98.00 annually; $78 to members of AAHE, AIR, or AERA; and $68 to ASHE members. All foreign subscribers must include an additional $10 per series year for postage.

To order, use the order form on the last page of this book. Regular prices are as follows:

Series	Price	Series	Price
1993	$18.00	1985 to 87	$10.00
1990 to 92	$17.00	1983 and 84	$7.50
1988 and 89	$15.00	before 1983	$6.50

Discounts on non-subscription orders:
* Bookstores, and current members of AERA, AIR, AAHE and ASHE, receive a 25% discount.
* Bulk: For non-bookstore, non-member orders of 10 or more books, deduct 10%

Shipping costs are as follows:
* U.S. address: 5% of invoice subtotal for orders over $50.00; $2.50 for each order with an invoice subtotal of $50.00 or less.
* Foreign: $2.50 per book.

All orders under $45.00 must be prepaid. Make check payable to ASHE-ERIC. For Visa or MasterCard, include card number, expiration date and signature.

Address order to
ASHE-ERIC Higher Education Reports
The George Washington University
1 Dupont Circle, Suite 630
Washington, DC 20036
Or phone (202) 296-2597
Write or call for a complete catalog.

1993 ASHE-ERIC Higher Education Reports

1. The Department Chair: New Roles, Responsibilities and Challenges
   Alan T. Seagren, John W. Creswell, and Daniel W. Wheeler

2. Sexual Harassment in Higher Education: From Conflict to Community
   Robert O. Riggs, Patricia H. Murrell, and JoAnn C. Cutting

1992 ASHE-ERIC Higher Education Reports

1. The Leadership Compass: Values and Ethics in Higher Education
   John R. Wilcox and Susan L. Ebbs

2. Preparing for a Global Community: Achieving an International Perspective in Higher Education
   Sarah M. Pickert

3. Quality: Transforming Postsecondary Education
   Ellen Earle Chaffee and Lawrence A. Sherr

4. Faculty Job Satisfaction: Women and Minorities in Peril
   Martha Wingard Tack and Carol Logan Patitu

5. Reconciling Rights and Responsibilities of Colleges and Students: Offensive Speech, Assembly, Drug Testing, and Safety
   Annette Gibbs

6. Creating Distinctiveness: Lessons from Uncommon Colleges and Universities
   Barbara K. Townsend, L. Jackson Newell, and Michael D. Wiese

7. Instituting Enduring Innovations: Achieving Continuity of Change in Higher Education
   Barbara K. Curry

8. Crossing Pedagogical Oceans: International Teaching Assistants in U.S. Undergraduate Education
   Rosslyn M. Smith, Patricia Byrd, Gayle L. Nelson, Ralph Pat Barrett, and Janet C. Constantinides

1991 ASHE-ERIC Higher Education Reports

1. Active Learning: Creating Excitement in the Classroom
   Charles C. Bonwell and James A. Eison

2. Realizing Gender Equality in Higher Education: The Need to Integrate Work/Family Issues
   Nancy Hensel

3. Academic Advising for Student Success: A System of Shared Responsibility
   Susan H. Frost

4. Cooperative Learning: Increasing College Faculty Instructional Productivity
   David W. Johnson, Roger T. Johnson, and Karl A. Smith

5. High School–College Partnerships: Conceptual Models, Programs, and Issues
   Arthur Richard Greenberg

6. Meeting the Mandate: Renewing the College and Departmental Curriculum
   William Toombs and William Tierney

7. Faculty Collaboration: Enhancing the Quality of Scholarship and Teaching
   Ann E. Austin and Roger G. Baldwin

8. Strategies and Consequences: Managing the Costs in Higher Education
   John S. Waggaman

1990 ASHE-ERIC Higher Education Reports

1. The Campus Green: Fund Raising in Higher Education
   Barbara E. Brittingham and Thomas R. Pezzullo

2. The Emeritus Professor: Old Rank - New Meaning
   James E. Mauch, Jack W. Birch, and Jack Matthews

3. "High Risk" Students in Higher Education: Future Trends
   Dionne J. Jones and Betty Collier Watson

4. Budgeting for Higher Education at the State Level: Enigma, Paradox, and Ritual
   Daniel T. Layzell and Jan W. Lyddon

5. Proprietary Schools: Programs, Policies, and Prospects
   John B. Lee and Jamie P. Merisotis

6. College Choice: Understanding Student Enrollment Behavior
   Michael B. Paulsen

7. Pursuing Diversity: Recruiting College Minority Students
   Barbara Astone and Elsa Nuñez-Wormack

8. Social Consciousness and Career Awareness: Emerging Link in Higher Education
   John S. Swift, Jr.

1989 ASHE-ERIC Higher Education Reports

1. Making Sense of Administrative Leadership: The 'L' Word in Higher Education
   Estela M. Bensimon, Anna Neumann, and Robert Birnbaum

2. Affirmative Rhetoric, Negative Action: African-American and Hispanic Faculty at Predominantly White Universities
   Valora Washington and William Harvey

3. Postsecondary Developmental Programs: A Traditional Agenda with New Imperatives
   Louise M. Tomlinson

4. The Old College Try: Balancing Athletics and Academics in Higher Education
   John R. Thelin and Lawrence L. Wiseman

5. The Challenge of Diversity: Involvement or Alienation in the Academy?
   Daryl G. Smith

6. Student Goals for College and Courses: A Missing Link in Assessing and Improving Academic Achievement
   Joan S. Stark, Kathleen M. Shaw, and Malcolm A. Lowther

7. The Student as Commuter: Developing a Comprehensive Institutional Response
   Barbara Jacoby

8. Renewing Civic Capacity: Preparing College Students for Service and Citizenship
   Suzanne W. Morse

1988 ASHE-ERIC Higher Education Reports

1. The Invisible Tapestry: Culture in American Colleges and Universities
   George D. Kuh and Elizabeth J. Whitt

2. Critical Thinking: Theory, Research, Practice, and Possibilities
   Joanne Gainen Kurfiss

3. Developing Academic Programs: The Climate for Innovation
   Daniel T. Seymour

4. Peer Teaching: To Teach is To Learn Twice
   Neal A. Whitman

5. Higher Education and State Governments: Renewed Partnership, Cooperation, or Competition?
   Edward R. Hines

6. Entrepreneurship and Higher Education: Lessons for Colleges, Universities, and Industry
   James S. Fairweather

7. Planning for Microcomputers in Higher Education: Strategies for the Next Generation
   Reynolds Ferrante, John Hayman, Mary Susan Carlson, and Harry Phillips

8. The Challenge for Research in Higher Education: Harmonizing Excellence and Utility
   Alan W. Lindsay and Ruth T. Neumann

1987 ASHE-ERIC Higher Education Reports

1. Incentive Early Retirement Programs for Faculty: Innovative Responses to a Changing Environment
   Jay L. Chronister and Thomas R. Kepple, Jr.

2. Working Effectively with Trustees: Building Cooperative Campus Leadership
   Barbara E. Taylor

3. Formal Recognition of Employer-Sponsored Instruction: Conflict and Collegiality in Postsecondary Education
   Nancy S. Nash and Elizabeth M. Hawthorne

4. Learning Styles: Implications for Improving Educational Practices
   Charles S. Claxton and Patricia H. Murrell

5. Higher Education Leadership: Enhancing Skills through Professional Development Programs
   Sharon A. McDade

6. Higher Education and the Public Trust: Improving Stature in Colleges and Universities
   Richard L. Alfred and Julie Weissman

7. College Student Outcomes Assessment: A Talent Development Perspective
   Maryann Jacobi, Alexander Astin, and Frank Ayala, Jr.

8. Opportunity from Strength: Strategic Planning Clarified with Case Examples
   Robert G. Cope

1986 ASHE-ERIC Higher Education Reports

1. Post-tenure Faculty Evaluation: Threat or Opportunity?
   Christine M. Licata

2. Blue Ribbon Commissions and Higher Education: Changing Academe from the Outside
   Janet R. Johnson and Laurence R. Marcus

3. Responsive Professional Education: Balancing Outcomes and Opportunities
   Joan S. Stark, Malcolm A. Lowther, and Bonnie M.K. Hagerty

4. Increasing Students' Learning: A Faculty Guide to Reducing Stress among Students
   Neal A. Whitman, David C. Spendlove, and Claire H. Clark

5. Student Financial Aid and Women: Equity Dilemma?
   Mary Moran

6. The Master's Degree: Tradition, Diversity, Innovation
   Judith S. Glazer

7. The College, the Constitution, and the Consumer Student: Implications for Policy and Practice
   Robert M. Hendrickson and Annette Gibbs

8. Selecting College and University Personnel: The Quest and the Question
   Richard A. Kaplowitz

1985 ASHE-ERIC Higher Education Reports

1. Flexibility in Academic Staffing: Effective Policies and Practices
   Kenneth P. Mortimer, Marque Bagshaw, and Andrew T. Masland

2. Associations in Action: The Washington, D.C. Higher Education Community
   Harland G. Bloland

3. And on the Seventh Day: Faculty Consulting and Supplemental Income
   Carol M. Boyer and Darrell R. Lewis

4. Faculty Research Performance: Lessons from the Sciences and Social Sciences
   John W. Creswell

5. Academic Program Review: Institutional Approaches, Expectations, and Controversies
   Clifton F. Conrad and Richard F. Wilson

6. Students in Urban Settings: Achieving the Baccalaureate Degree
   Richard C. Richardson, Jr. and Louis W. Bender

7. Serving More Than Students: A Critical Need for College Student Personnel Services
   Peter H. Garland

8. Faculty Participation in Decision Making: Necessity or Luxury?
   Carol E. Floyd

*Out-of-print. Available through EDRS. Call 1-800-443-ERIC.